Village '
—————— in -
NORF(

Village Walks
in
NORFOLK

Liz Moynihan

COUNTRYSIDE BOOKS
NEWBURY, BERKSHIRE

First published 1998
© Liz Moynihan 1998

COUNTRYSIDE BOOKS
3 Catherine Road
Newbury, Berkshire

ISBN 1 85306 516 1

Designed by Graham Whiteman
Photographs by the author
Maps by Sarah Talks
Illustrations by Trevor Yorke

Front cover photo of Elsing Mill
taken by Rod Edwards

Produced through MRM Associates Ltd., Reading
Printed by J. W. Arrowsmith Ltd., Bristol

Contents

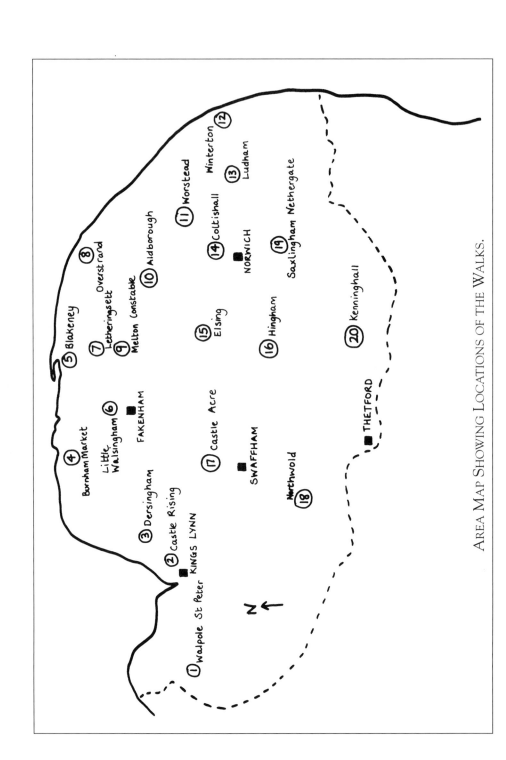

AREA MAP SHOWING LOCATIONS OF THE WALKS.

WALK

To Aplhaeus

Publisher's Note

We hope that you obtain considerable enjoyment from this book; great care has been taken in its preparation. Although at the time of publication all routes followed public rights of way or permitted paths, diversion orders can be made and permissions withdrawn.

We cannot of course be held responsible for such diversion orders and any inaccuracies in the text which result from these or any other changes to the routes nor any damage which might result from walkers trespassing on private property. We are anxious though that all details covering the walks are kept up to date and would therefore welcome information from readers which would be relevant to future editions.

Introduction

I may be biased but I can't think of any other county in Britain which has as many attractive villages as Norfolk. The appeal of a village lies not only in its position in the landscape, its wealth of natural features, its historical links, and its people, but above all in its architecture which is the first impression that a visitor receives. Because of difficulties of access, Norfolk village architecture relies very much on local materials which differ across the breadth of the county. There is much use of stone of various colours from creamy white chalk blocks to warm orange soft stone and darker brown carr stone in the north-west of the county. Flint in the form of rounded pebbles, rough chunks or smoothly worked is much in evidence as is mellow red brick and rough cob. Some buildings can be an amalgamation of all types. Almost everywhere are the soft orange tones of pantiles for the roofs or maybe thatch in areas which have easy access to reeds. Add this domestic munificence to the grandeur of the ecclesiastical architecture found in abundance even in the tiniest hamlet and you have a recipe for infinite variety and total delight.

The task of picking out just a few of these many lovely villages was an almost impossible one. I have tried therefore to give a taste of everything. There are some well known villages which simply cannot be left out, there are pretty villages which give a flavour of different parts of the county, there are one or two not so pretty villages which have other important features, and some small out of the way hamlets which hardly qualify for the name of village at all. I am sure you will enjoy discovering them and exploring the surrounding countryside on these walks.

Some paths can be quite overgrown and rough, so please do wear suitable footwear, and trousers and long sleeves. Villages are small places with narrow roads and lanes so please park considerately. Don't take up space outside churches if a service is likely, and only use pub car parks with permission. Details of pubs and cafes are given and most are happy for you to use their car park provided you patronise the establishment. The walks are circular, using lanes and ancient paths which pass landscape and historical features closely linked to each village. They vary in length from 2 to 6½ miles and I have often indicated short cuts for those with limited time to spare – I have occasionally, too, suggested extensions for those who can't tear themselves away. Although a sketch map is provided the relevant Ordnance Survey map will add to your enjoyment and I have given the Landranger 1:50 000 sheet number in each case. Finally, there are details of other places of interest in the vicinity which could be included in a really enjoyable day out for all the family.

Liz Moynihan

WALPOLE ST PETER

Length: 2 miles

Getting there: Walpole St Peter is a mile down a turning north-west off the A47 road between Wisbech and King's Lynn.	Parking: Near the beginning of School Lane. There is alternative parking near Walpole St Andrew church.	Map: OS Landranger 131 Boston and Spalding area (GR 504166).

The glory of the villages of Walpole St Peter and neighbouring Walpole St Andrew lies in their magnificent churches which encapsulate the whole history of the locality. The special character of this marshland area in the north of the county towards the Lincolnshire border results from the land having been wrested from the sea by the building of dykes and sea walls going back beyond Roman times. Later in the Middle Ages the wealth of the area was generated by extensive sheep farming when lavish endowments resulted in magnificent church architectural work.

At Walpole St Peter, the 'Cathedral of the Fens' is much visited by those with an interest in architecture and history, including members of the royal family from nearby Sandringham. The framed signatures from the visitors' book in the church themselves provide a history lesson. Social history is reflected in the pattens (iron overshoes to keep the wearer out of the mud) hanging outside the church door with the old notice requesting that all persons take off their pattens at the church door, and the portable covered shelter like a sentry box to protect the parson when conducting funerals. The main parts of the church were built after the Black Death in 1348, which halted all public works, when the agricultural emphasis changed to sheep farming which led to the prosperity reflected in the church building. Later, in the early 17th century, the pulpit and font cover were donated, then in about 1630 the unusual western screen and nave pews were added. The lovely carved ends of the benches in the south aisle are 15th century. The remains of the rood screen has painted panels of saints and there are beautiful carved stone canopies over the choir stalls, and some medieval glass. Rich additions are the medieval brass lectern and a vast brass chandelier of 1701. Alec Clifton-

Taylor, the architectural historian, called it 'probably the finest church in England'. Outside the eye is drawn to the tower of 1300, the only part of the church left standing when a flood breached the protecting sea walls, and the pretty bellcote with its sanctus bell. Look for the strange figure in the corner of the chancel and north aisle, possibly Hickathrift, a local mystical figure.

The villages are associated with the great Walpole family who lived here in Norman times and who later had their seat at Houghton Hall further to the east and produced Britain's first prime minister. The walk goes along an ancient path between the two churches and returns along lanes. The two villages used to be linked by scattered smallholdings (flowers, fruit and vegetables, some under glass) but although now almost every space seems to have been infilled with modern housing, you can still get some of the unique flavour of this fenland area. A ¼ mile to the north of the route of the walk, down a lane opposite Walpole St Andrew church, is the ancient sea bank dating from Roman times – one of the earliest fenland reclamation schemes, stretching from the Wash to Wisbech. A little further north is King John bank where rumour has it that the King's treasure was lost.

THE WALK
❶ Follow School Lane as it bends round through houses and cottages and carry on into the churchyard of Walpole St Peter church. Bear immediately right to follow a path which leads through a beautiful tunnel (The Chase) under the chancel of the church with lovely carved vaulting and

War memorial in the churchyard at Walpole St Andrew.

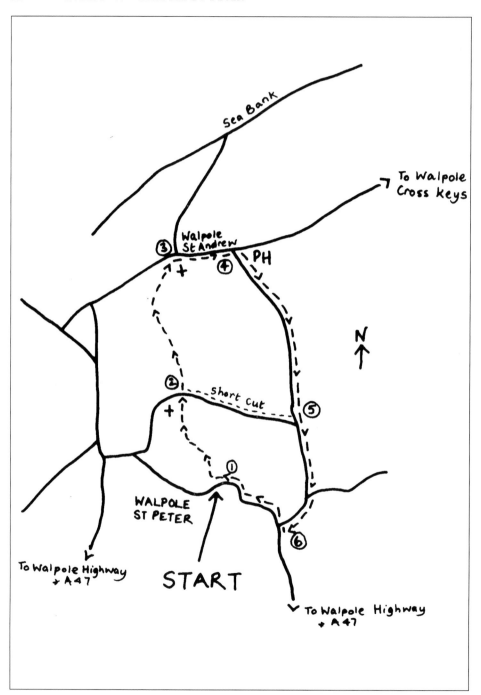

rings on the right for tethering horses. This is part of an old path which leads straight to Walpole St Andrew church less than a mile to the north. Follow this path out of the churchyard onto a road.

❷ Cross and go along a footpath, passing old farm buildings on the right and the restored Manor House on the left. When the path comes out onto an estate road, go ahead for a short distance and join a metalled footpath on the other side. This passes modern houses and a playing field on the right and then continues through rough ground to another estate of modern houses. Continue on past the modern primary school and then later the old yellow brick school on the right. At a junction bear right to Kirk Road and turn right to walk through the churchyard of Walpole St Andrew, looked after by the Redundant Churches Trust. This huge 15th-century church has a brick tower with turrets housing the rood stairs and a cell in the south-west buttress possibly used by an anchorite. Inside are shepherds' crooks from the Shepherds Club founded in 1841 as a benevolent society and a Jacobean pulpit fitted with an hourglass on a stand. The path through the churchyard passes an interesting bronze war memorial decorated with farm animals and an inscription, 'ye that live on mid English pastures green, remember us and think what might have been'.

❸ Turn left out of the churchyard to meet the road and then turn right along the

---

PLACES of INTEREST

Other great fenland churches at **West Walton, Wiggenhall St Mary, Terrington St Clement** and **Tilney All Saints**. The **African Violet Centre,** nursery displays, tearoom and shop at Terrington St Clement. The **Fenland Aviation Museum** at West Walton, south-west of Walpole St Peter, (telephone: 01945 463996) has aviation and related relics of the Second World War.

---

road, passing a few houses.

❹ At a road junction with the Princess Victoria on the corner, turn right along a minor road (with a church sign) and walk for some distance without turning off, through housing and then more open countryside with views across on the right to the great church at Walpole St Peter.

❺ At a T junction bear left (following another church sign), ignoring Church Road to the right (suitable for a short cut if required), and walk through smallholding territory marked by glasshouses behind modern infilling. Ignore a turn to the left and further on another one to the left. Soon after this the road bears right to meet a T junction.

❻ Turn right (still following the church sign) along Walnut Road, another mix of old cottages with newer infill. Carry on until the road bears sharply to the left where, at a grassy triangle graced by an old walnut tree, you come to School Lane and the parking place.

CASTLE RISING

Length: 5 miles

Getting there: The village is a few miles north of King's Lynn, just west of the A149 between King's Lynn and Hunstanton.

Parking: In the street near the church and almshouses or in the English Heritage car park if visting the castle.

Map: OS Landranger 132 North West Norfolk (GR 666248).

Castle Rising is a village that has it all. As well as its magnificent castle with the ruins of the original Norman church embedded in its embankment, you will find the delightful 17th-century Hospital of the Holy and Undivided Trinity built as almshouses by Henry Howard, Earl of Northampton for needy women of good character, an unusual 12th-century church, an old market cross on the green and beautiful old houses, cottages and barns mostly built from soft-red brick. Add to this a pretty post office which does refreshments, inside or in the attractive garden, and a successful pub and you couldn't want for more. The view from the

FOOD and DRINK

The comfortable Black Horse Inn has a varied menu (telephone: 01553 631225). The Farmers Arms inn and restaurant at the Knight's Hill Village hotel complex, South Wootton (telephone: 01553 675566) has real ale and guest beers and good food. Castle Rising post office does coffees, teas and light lunches (except Wednesday afternoons).

huge earthworks surrounding the remains of the castle is amazing. It stretches over marshlands to the nearby Wash and inland over the village and the distant woods of the Sandringham estate. The sea seems so close that you can well imagine ships coming into port here up the Babingley river which was tidal in earlier times, giving rise to the old rhyme:

Rising was a sea-port town when Lynn was but a marsh
Now Lynn it is a sea-port town and Rising fares the worse.

The countryside you will walk through is as varied and delightful as the village. The route leaves the village via Night Marsh and the ruins of St Felix church, then turns into the lovely woods and heathland of Wootton Carr and Ling Common. The wooded path continues over a golf course to return to Castle Rising along a tiny lane giving views over the castle mound.

THE WALK
❶ From the church and almshouses continue down the lane away from the village centre, passing playing fields on the right and the old rectory on the left. Near a

brick cottage continue on through wooden gates along a leafy lane. As the lane bears to the right turn left down a bank along a narrow path which leads along the edge of a field. There are views over Night Marsh to derelict St Felix church on the right and on the left back to St Lawrence church at Castle Rising. At a wooden footpath signpost turn left along a broad lane with fields on the right and parkland on the left. The track then passes pretty cottages and bears right.

❷ At the road junction ignore the road to the left (except as a short detour to view the splendid market cross on the green) and carry on along a lane, passing attractive houses. At a grassy triangle the road bears to the left. Take the wide track rightish marked by a wooden footpath signpost, go through wooden gates and by a big barn on the right take a track to the left, walking along the edge of a meadow bordered by a hedge and trees. Bear left near a cottage on the right (wooden footpath signpost) and shortly veer off the

PLACES of INTEREST

Nearby King's Lynn is a most interesting town architecturally and has several attractions including **Lynn Museum**, the **Old Gaol House Museum**, **Town House Museum of Lynn Life** and **True's Yard**. For details ring the Tourist Office (telephone: 01553 763044). **Congham Hall herb garden** in the grounds of a hotel, south of the A148 Cromer road (telephone: 01485 600250). **Roydon Common**, also reached from the A148, where you can have a walk through a Norfolk Wildlife Trust reserve interesting for wetland plants and also those of dry acid heath. Also belonging to the Norfolk Wildlife Trust is **East Winch Common**, south-east of King's Lynn.

The almshouses in Castle Rising.

main track along a narrow, overgrown path marked by a wooden footpath signpost. In summer months the bracken is shoulder high but the path is obvious and well trodden, passing for some distance through this attractive common area (Wootton Carr) dotted with silver birch. Come out onto Ling Common Road.

❸ Cross over the road, going a few paces to the right, and go into the woodland of Ling Common at a wooden footpath signpost. Keep straight ahead along a fairly wide path, ignoring the branch to the left. The path goes along near the edge of the wood with houses visible on the right. At a junction with a path going to the left, keep on ahead with a ditch or stream on the

right. Cross over a small wooden footbridge near a path to the right leading to houses. Ignore this and continue straight on. Cross over another footbridge and continue on through the swampy woodland away from the houses. Cross another little bridge and soon after this you come to a broad path going off to the left just before yet another small bridge. Turn off to the left along this path and carry on where a small path comes in from the left. At another junction of small tracks by a wooden bridge cross this to the right and bear left along quite a major track with a waterway on the left. When the waterway bears off left, keep on along the track and at another major junction of paths bear left. Where another path goes off to the right, bear left again, following along a ditch on the left. Keep on along this path, ignoring other small paths off. It meanders on, still following the ditch, until it comes out onto a road at a parking area almost opposite the entrance to a golf club.

❹ Turn right along the road for a fairly short distance and watch out for a narrow footpath going to the left (marked by an almost hidden wooden footpath signpost). Turn left along this often overgrown path through woodland alongside a wire fence

on the right and the golf course on the left. The path keeps straight on ahead, sometimes opening out to cross over part of the golf course, finally making for the back of a white notice where it becomes very narrow through woodland, then an open field through the fringe of woodland on the right. The path bears sharply to the right to come out at the main A148 road.

❺ Turn left along the wide verge and walk about ¼ mile, passing a pair of carr stone cottages.

❻ As you come up to the Knight's Hill hotel complex on the right, turn left along a narrow lane which runs for about a mile, heading for Castle Rising with occasional views across the fields to the castle. After passing derelict barns, you come to the entrance to the English Heritage car park on the left through which there is access to the castle built by William d'Albini (whose family came from France with William the Conqueror) in the 12th century. Queen Isabella, mother of Edward III, was banished here after her involvement in the murder of Edward II and lived in the massive keep for 27 years. The estate then belonged to the Black Prince, but was later given by Henry VIII to the Duke of Norfolk.

If visiting the castle you can afterwards continue down the path onto the village street where you turn left. Otherwise continue down the lane to a crossroads and bear left. Continue along the road, passing pretty cottages and bearing right to another crossroads. Continue straight on to visit the church of St Lawrence, mostly rebuilt in Victorian times when the saddle roof was added to the tower, but with a Norman west front and Norman font decorated with cats' faces (indicating that it came from the earlier church of St Felix), and the village green with its market cross; otherwise turn right, passing the post office. Next door on the corner is the Black Horse pub and over the road the West Norfolk Arts Centre which does residential and day courses in the Old Schoolhouse. Note the old lamp standards along the road here. Bear left at the corner and where the more major road bears right continue straight on back to the parking near the almshouses. The chapel here can be visited on Tuesday, Thursday and Saturday from 10 am to 12 noon and 2 pm to 6 pm. On special days the occupants wear their uniform of red cloaks and conical hats.

DERSINGHAM

Length: 5 miles

Getting there: Dersingham is about 6 miles north of King's Lynn, signposted along the B1440 from a roundabout on the A149. Turn right shortly after the roundabout along Heath Road	near the Dersingham village sign. **Parking:** Look for the unmarked parking area on the left about halfway along Heath Road	almost opposite a bungalow. There is alternative parking at Sandringham. **Map:** OS Landranger 132 North West Norfolk (GR 688298).

This attractive walk makes the most of the links between the ancient village of Dersingham and the nearby Sandringham estate. In medieval times Dersingham (now 2½ miles from the sea) was a port and its fishermen were granted the freedom of

FOOD and DRINK

The Gamekeeper's Lodge (freehouse), a real country bar and restaurant with a carvery on Friday, Saturday and Sunday (telephone: 01485 543514); the Feathers (telephone: 01485 540207); the Coach and Horses (telephone: 01485 540391. There is also a restaurant near the car park at Sandringham.

the seas by Henry VI. Just after the Norman Conquest it had seven manors including Sandringham. The walk not only passes very ancient buildings such as the 15th-century church, on one boundary of which stands a splendid crow-stepped barn of 1671, and the Old Hall which incorporates part of the 17th-century manor of the Pells, but also Victorian and Edwardian houses and villas. These were built after 1862 when the nearby Sandringham estate was bought for the Prince of Wales (later Edward VII). Local carr stone is much in evidence, often mixed with other local materials to provide a very lively architecture. The village boasts a wide selection of shops and businesses, some with royal warrants including a butcher's shop in Chapel Road. In the same road is a pottery and art gallery in beautiful converted carr stone buildings.

The walk begins by passing through Dersingham Common – a sandy heath with silver birches, small oaks, some beech and fir and lovely wild flowers – to reach the woods of the Sandringham estate, part of which is run as a country park with walks and nature trails which can be used to extend the walk, and a restaurant and visitor centre where tickets can be bought to visit Sandringham House and garden.

Back in the village, the walker climbs gently up Mill Road with its flowery verges to a pretty group of buildings where a windmill once stood. Here there are outstanding views towards the Wash and into Lincolnshire, over marshes where a duck decoy once stood and over the vast woods of Sandringham.

THE WALK

❶ Cross over the lane from the layby and take the track (wooden signpost) into the common – a delightful sandy, brackeny heath dotted with a variety of trees. Go ahead along the more main track without turning off on any lesser track. Continue on over an open space with rustic benches, ignoring all side paths. The trees close in and the path curves uphill. When the path forks, take a slightly smaller path towards the right, and cross a plank bridge. At a crossroads of paths, go right into a clearing with magnificent firs among the other trees. Turn right along this broad track and then very shortly bear left along another broad path. Come out onto a little roadway which leads to the parking area at

PLACES of INTEREST

Dersingham Pottery and Gallery in Chapel Road. Sandringham House, grounds, museum and country park, belonging to the royal family since 1861. Open except when the royal family is in residence, (telephone: 01553 772675). Wolferton Station Museum with its royal connections (telephone: 01485 540674). Caley Mill, home of Norfolk lavender, with its gardens, tours, shop and tearoom is up the A149 to the north of Dersingham (telephone: 01485 570384). Further north there is Hunstanton Sealife Centre (telephone: 01485 533576).

A crow-stepped barn in the village.

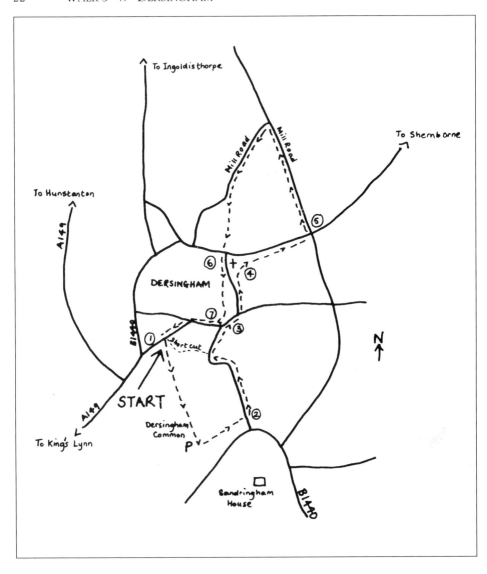

Sandringham. Turn left and walk along the roadway here. Turn right to visit the house, the restaurant, the shop or toilets; otherwise turn left through wooden barriers along a grassy ride through the woods to come out near the beautiful wrought iron Norwich Gates (given as a

wedding present to the Prince and Princess of Wales in 1863 by the County of Norfolk and City of Norwich) over to the right.

❷ Turn left along the broad verge and avenue of young copper beeches lining the road. In summer the air is heavy with the scent of the huge limes whose branches dip down to the ground like skirts. Continue on until the broad sward ends at a track on the left. Cross the road and continue on along the pavement as the roads bends to the left, looking down on Dersingham in the valley ahead. Ignore a broad metalled track to the left and carry on, bearing right again on the approach to the village. The green path which goes to the left between the fences of fields would be a short cut back to your car – it bears left and then right again to skirt the edge of the common and come out near the parking area.

For the complete walk, carry on into Dersingham past late Victorian and Edwardian brick or carr stone villas, and go downhill to the road junction. On the far side is a book and craft shop which serves refreshments.

❸ Bear right at the junction, passing the fine carr stone Feathers hotel and pub, which has a pleasant garden to one side backing onto a large playing field and the Prince of Wales' feathers displayed outside. Pass the old school on the right, now Dersingham Centre for Youth and Community. Cross over Dodshill Road and continue on, passing the Coach and Horses on the other side of the road. At the corner of the churchyard, bear right up Church Lane, passing the lovely barns of Manor Farm on the right with views of the church and tithe barn on the left.

❹ At the next T junction turn right up Shernborne Road, passing some large houses on the left.

The ornate chest to be found in Dersingham church.

❺ At the top of the road turn left into Mill Road, a lane with wide verges going uphill between hedges towards a group of former mill buildings. At the top the lane carries on to Ingoldisthorpe. Turn left off it, passing pretty Mill Cottage. Follow the wall of Mill House round to the left and carry on downhill, again with impressive views. The lane bends slightly to the left and passes Hill House Farm. As the road bends to the right go off a little to the left along a grassy track called Sugar Lane. Where the lane turns left into the yard of a house go ahead along a narrow grassy track, passing houses, gardens and old walls. The track was virtually taken over by the large leaves of butterbur when I walked. The path, now cobbled, meets the road. Turn left here to visit Dersingham Pottery in Chapel Road; further on is the old chapel itself and the butcher's shop graced with the royal insignia.

❻ To finish this walk turn left and then right at a road junction by 16th-century Game-keeper's Lodge Hotel, formerly the Dersingham Hall Hotel, with its crow-stepped gables. To the left are pretty carr stone cottages on Shernborne Road. Continue along Manor Road, passing the magnificent old tithe barn and the splendid 15th-century church of St Nicholas with its hammer beam roof, 14th-century carved chest with emblems of the evangelists, and painted screen. An unusual incised black marble tomb is dated 1607 and a coffin lid goes back to the 12th century. Opposite the church is a car park and hall. Just inside the car park, cross a stile and go left into a field, crossing a ditch and continuing on into the recreation area. Skirt round the edge of this to the left and leave via a broad green ride at the end of the Feathers' garden. Turn right and continue on the pavement along Manor Road.

❼ Pass the junction with the Sandringham road where the walk entered Dersingham and continue on along Manor Road. The exuberant Forester's Hall on the right is now a carpet showroom. Cross over a side turning opposite some shops and then after Senter's Lane on the left, turn left into Heath Road to go back to the parking area. Further on along Manor Road just before its junction with the Lynn road is a row of charming cottages, formerly the old manor of West Hall.

BURNHAM MARKET

Length: 4 miles

Getting there: Burnham Market is south of the A149 between Hunstanton and Wells.

Parking: Adjacent to the green in the centre of the village.

Map: OS Landranger 132 North West Norfolk (GR 832422).

This large, successful village is one of the most attractive in Norfolk. The wide central green is lined with beautiful houses, mostly dating from the late 17th or 18th century, sometimes with earlier buildings behind the façades. Some house interesting shops and businesses of all kinds. The streets leading from the centre have equally attractive but smaller cottages with a range of ages and styles whilst on the outskirts lie the large manor houses and farms. It is the centre of the original seven Burnhams – originally Norton, Overy, Westgate, Sutton, Ulph, St Edmonds and St Andrews. The last two have disappeared, being replaced by Deepdale, and perhaps the most famous of all, Burnham Thorpe, where Nelson was born. A stream called the Goose Beck runs underground and occasionally floods,

FOOD and DRINK

The Hoste Arms (telephone: 01328 738257), the Lord Nelson (telephone: 01328 738321), Gurney's Cafe (telephone: 01328 738967) and Fishes Restaurant (telephone: 01328 738588).

running through the Market Place and creating fords on all the roads. There are still two churches, belonging to the parishes of Westgate and Ulph.

The walk goes on to explore the countryside outside Burnham Market, visiting Burnham Overy Town and passing the unusual church, St Clement's, with its Norman tower surmounted by a cupola and weathervane. Not far from St Margaret's church, Burnham Norton, with its Saxon round tower standing on a ridge overlooking the sea, are the remains of a Carmelite friary founded in 1242 with a fine 14th-century gatehouse. The nearby village houses have disappeared and from the ridge there are views over present-day Burnham Norton on the edge of the marshes, and over Burnham Overy Staithe, the port of the Burnhams, with its fine 18th-century watermill and landmark windmill of 1816. Nelson learned to sail here.

THE WALK

❶ With your back to the Hoste Arms, named after one of Nelson's captains, Sir William Hoste, turn left and walk along the edge of the Market Place, passing Fishes Restaurant. Pass tiny Herrings Lane and then various shops. With early 18th-century Barclay's Bank on the corner, carry on along North Street, passing the neatly cobbled early 19th-century NatWest Bank and various shops in interesting buildings such as the brick chapel of about 1830 and the warehouse on the other side of the road, then cottages and houses old and new. On the right is the cobbled old school and then the church of All Saints, Sutton and Ulph, dating back to the late 12th century. Pass a left turn to Brancaster and Hunstanton down Bellamy's Lane, then a sharp right fork which would take you back to the Market Place. Keep on ahead here along the B1155 to Cromer and Wells.

❷ Turn right along Joan Shorts Lane out into countryside. At a small junction with a bungalow on the corner turn left down a concrete drive leading past the sewage works on the right and on to a narrow footpath through woods, once the track of an old railway. Cross over the river Burn.

❸ Look out for a track on the left opposite two big ash trees. Follow this along the edge of a field, carrying on into another field, and before long the path meets a road on the outskirts of Burnham Overy Town. Turn left along the road, passing a lovely farm barn and house on the left and St Clement's church on the right to reach a

PLACES of INTEREST

Holkham Hall and gardens and **Holkham Bygones** museum. **Holkham National Nature Reserve** to the north-east and **Scolt Head Island National Nature Reserve** to the north. The ruins of Augustinian **Creake Abbey** (English Heritage), are just off the B1355 to the south and **Houghton Hall**, built for Robert Walpole, is further south.

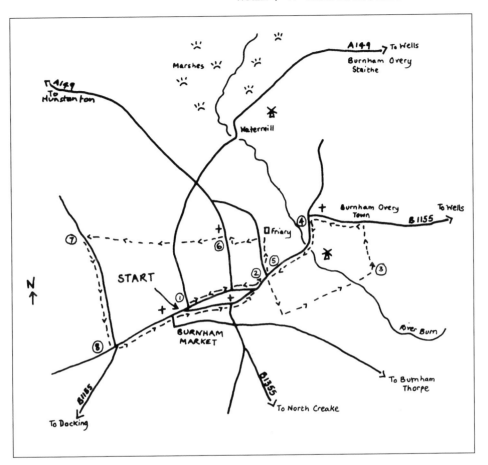

road junction by a row of attractive cottages.

❹ Turn left, signposted back into Burnham Market, and walk along the pavement, passing a mill complex where the road crosses the river Burn.

❺ At the next junction turn right up Friar's Lane to the remains of the Carmelite friary of 1242 which was dissolved in 1538. Turn your back on the unfortunately sited school for a picturesque view of the ruins with St Clement's church in the back-ground. Retrace your steps, then just next to the school grounds turn right up a signposted path to reach Bellamy's Lane, which could be a short cut back to Burnham Market.

❻ For the main walk, turn right for a short distance to Burnham Norton church from which there are spectacular views. Just before the church turn left along a broad signposted track which reaches another lane with another possible short cut, left.

View of Burnham Overy Town's unusual church, with its Norman tower.

For the main walk, go right for a few paces then turn left down another signposted broad track, passing some large houses and then Mill Wood on the left to reach Whiteway Road.

❼ Turn left along this, back into Burnham Market, enjoying the views of rolling countryside and then imposing Westgate Hall, designed by Sir John Soane in 1783 on the left.

❽ At the B1155 turn left, passing a pond, a modern surgery and then St Mary Westgate with its 14th-century flint tower topped with fine carvings. Walk along the right-hand side of the green, passing St Henry's Roman Catholic church and beautiful 18th and early 19th-century

houses and some shops. Behind the post office is the Gazebo, possibly built as a smuggler's lookout with tunnels in the cellars. Continue on into Front Street, again a charming mix of buildings, to reach the Lord Nelson pub. Then return to Market Place back along Front Street or North Street.

BLAKENEY
Length: 4½ miles

Getting there: Blakeney is on the A149 coast road halfway between Wells-next-the-Sea and Sheringham.	Parking: Pay car park on the Carnser (or hard) near the water (free to National Trust members) with toilets nearby. More parking off High Street or	at the village hall near the main road. Map: OS Landranger 133 North East Norfolk (GR 029442).

Two narrow streets of quaint houses, many built of flint or large round pebbles with mellow pantiled roofs, wind down to meet at the harbour in Blakeney which is still a busy scene of flapping sails, tinging halyards and launching trolleys when the tide is high. In medieval times Blakeney was a prosperous fishing and trading port

(local grain and salt from nearby Salt-house) as the converted warehouses in Ship Street and the wealth of curly Dutch gables and Flemish bricks testify. The Guildhall near the water with its 14th-century brick vaulted undercroft was probably a thriving merchant's house with basement storage or a fish market. In 1296

FOOD and DRINK

The Blakeney Hotel, built to replace a pub in the 1920s, has a restaurant open to non-residents (telephone: 01263 740797). You will also find the Manor Hotel, once the manor house, (telephone 01263 740376), the much smaller White Horse Hotel with its pleasant courtyard garden (telephone 01263 740574), the King's Arms, a traditional, family run freehouse which does food and accommodation (telephone 01263 740341) and the Moorings restaurant which does late breakfast, coffee, tea, light lunches and has an evening bistro.

a Carmelite friary was established to seaward of the windmill where Friary Farm now is. A brass plaque in the chancel of St Nicholas church commemorates John Calthorp, one of the friary's benefactors. The church, set back from the sea on a hill, is dedicated to the patron saint of fishing, and has a magnificent west tower built in 1435 with a smaller one at the east end used as a beacon to guide shipping. The 13th-century chancel has a groined roof with angels. The arcaded nave was rebuilt at the same time as the tower and has some medieval glass in the north aisle. The graveyard contains fine 17th and 18th-century gravestones.

Blakeney Point, a magical wilderness of ever shifting shingle banks, sand dunes, marshes and creeks juts out into the sea, providing a sanctuary for terns and other migrating birds, waders, water birds and seals as well as specialised flowers and plants. Owned by the National Trust, it can be reached by boat from Morston or Blakeney or on foot from Cley. The old lifeboat station on the point now serves refreshments. The pattern of the banks

and channels today is partly caused by the powerful local Calthorp family who over several centuries from the early 1600s built various sea walls in order to reclaim the marshes, causing the silting up of the estuary of the river Glaven leading to the decline of the once great port at nearby Wiveton. There are spectacular views over Blakeney Point from this walk which climbs up out of the village to reach Wiveton Downs, a high vantage point with a parking and a picnic area, before meandering downhill along an excellent track back into the village to meet the sea wall.

THE WALK

❶ Go up the High Street opposite the Carnser car park, noting the flood levels marked on the converted warehouse on the right. The High Street is a hotchpotch of shops, with the Moorings restaurant on the left and the White Horse Hotel on the opposite side, and as you go uphill there is a medley of cottages of all shapes and sizes including side alleys, or lokes, of terraced cottages hung with flowers. Some cottages have the plaque of the Blakeney Neighbourhood Housing Society which used a

PLACES of INTEREST

To the west, **Warham Iron Age fort** with double ramparts and a ditch, the extensive ruins and restored nave of Benedictine Binham Priory (English Heritage) and **Langham Glass**, down the B1388, where traditional glass is blown, with a shop and tearoom (telephone: 01328 830511). Ranged along the coast to the north you have **Cley Marshes** (Norfolk Wildlife Trust's premier bird reserve) as well as **Morston, Stiffkey** and **Salthouse Marshes**.

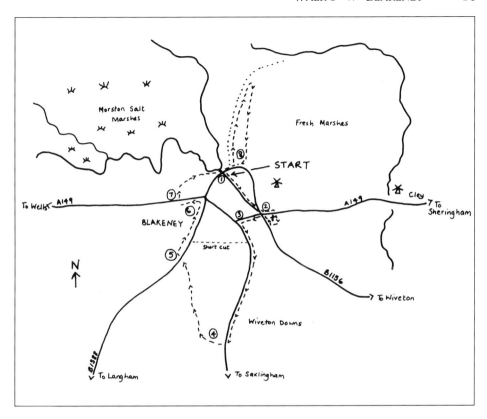

legacy to buy, restore and rent cottages to local people. The Methodist church of 1903 is made of dressed flints. Many of the pretty cottages have evocative names such as Jib Cottage and Bloater Cottage. Pass the British Legion hall where there is also a bowling green and car park. The High Street comes out onto the main A149 coast road.

❷ Turn left, crossing over the exit of Back Lane to walk a few yards to visit the splendid church of St Nicholas. On leaving the church continue up the path leading through the churchyard and follow it to the right coming out of a different gate through a car parking area with the Old Rectory opposite. Turn right down Wiveton Road (B1156), passing the junior school. At the crossroads turn left and walk along the pavement on the left, passing a war memorial outside Memorial Cottages.

❸ Turn left along Saxlingham Road.

For a short cut look out for a gravelled drive on the right just before the back of a road sign. The footpath signpost is almost hidden in the hedge on the right. Keep straight ahead down a stony drive between housing and continue on by a garage along a narrow fenced off path through bushes

The harbour.

and trees which eventually opens out into a field and passes along the back of bungalows to meet the Langham road. Turn right to rejoin the main walk.

For the main walk continue on up this lane, leaving housing and going out into the countryside. Pass Joe's Hill bungalow on the right. There are extensive views over the coast and Blakeney Point as the lane makes for the humps and bumps of the heathland of Wiveton Downs.

❹ Before this pass Pye's Farm on the left, and soon after the brow of the hill take the broad stony bridleway signposted to Blakeney to the right. As the path bends there are views over to the sea and the top of Blakeney church tower can be seen. Pass a bungalow on the right and go to the left of a farm gate. The track forks slightly to the left. Follow it as it narrows through a wild grassy area with white and pink foxgloves and campion in summer.

❺ Come out onto the Langham road (B1388) and turn right. Continue on into Blakeney, crossing over side roads and reaching the main road near the village hall on the right where there is free parking.

To curtail the walk, cross over the main road and continue back down to the quay along Westgate Street.

❻ To continue the main walk, turn left along the main road, walking along the pavement and passing modern housing on the left and Blakeney Garage and older cottages to the right. Look out for a footpath signposted between a garage and a cottage with a bold '56' on its front and turn right down the stony path here which becomes a narrow green track before reaching the bank of the Norfolk Coast Path.

❼ Turn right along this towards the masts of the harbour backed by a huddle of cottages dominated by Blakeney church tower. There are views of the marshes and creeks leading on to Blakeney Point on the left. Cross a grassy area alongside converted holiday cottages to bear right and pass through a gate near the creek which sweeps into Blakeney Quay. The Red House is on the right and Westgate Street bends up the hill just beyond it. Here are more shops including a splendid ship's chandlery on the left, the King's Arms pub with its date of 1760 written in tiles on the roof on the right. Bear left along the quay, passing Blakeney Hotel on the right to reach the Carnser and car park.

❽ To get a flavour of the marshes and a better view of Blakeney Point turn left opposite the toilets along the sea wall which divides the harbour from the grazing marshes beyond, passing the Horsepond with its wildfowl collection, and walk out along the sea wall, continuing along the bank until it turns right to carry on towards Cley. Here a secondary path goes out onto the marshes. Look for a stile on the right. Cross this and head back towards Blakeney across the grazing marsh, taking a line just to the right of the church tower. After passing the end of a stretch of water on the right head for a collection of gates and cross the stile to the right of them. There are views ahead of Friary Farm and its old wall (site of the ancient friary) and the base of the ruined windmill and to the left views of Cley and its restored windmill. Take a broad stony track which heads back to Blakeney, coming out to join the lane opposite the Manor Hote. Turn right back to the Carnser.

LITTLE WALSINGHAM

Length: 6½ miles

Getting there: Little Walsingham is on the B1105 midway between Fakenham and Wells-next-the-Sea.

Parking: Follow the signs to a large pay and display car park near the centre.

Map: OS Landranger 132 North West Norfolk (GR 934368).

Little Walsingham, a mile from its smaller neighbour Great Walsingham, is the site of England's great Anglican shrine, and a very important place of pilgrimage since medieval times. Early in the 11th century the lady of the manor, Richeldis de Faverches, had a vision of the Virgin Mary who ordered a chapel to be built at Walsingham. In the 14th century,

the Franciscans built their friary, the ruins of which still stand to the south of the village, while an Augustinian priory was founded on the chapel site, and the heyday of the pilgrimages had begun. A walk around the centre of Walsingham reveals a rich mix of buildings of all ages; even the loos built into the priory wall are listed! These are in the High Street near

---

FOOD and DRINK

The Robin Hood inn welcomes children and has a beer garden (telephone: 01328 820252); the Bull Inn is historically interesting with good beer and food, also accommodation (telephone: 01328 820333); the Black Lion Hotel (telephone: 01328 820235); Swallow's restaurant and guesthouse with home cooked food and snacks served all day (telephone: 01328 820555);Sharon's Pantry offers teas, coffees and light lunches (telephone 01328 820686); the Sue Ryder coffee/gift shop and accommodation (telephone: 01328 820622); the Old Bakehouse restaurant (only open evenings). There are also tearooms at the Slipper Chapel at Houghton of Giles (telephone: 01328 820495).

---

the 13th-century gateway to the Augustinian priory, ranged with other buildings from the 15th to the 18th century. Common Place is stuffed full of interest; there is the 16th-century Pump House, a fine 15th-century timbered building next to the Shrine Office, the Bull Inn which is also 15th century and has a racy history, and the Shirehall Museum and tourist office which houses a Georgian courthouse (1760–1820).

The walk leaves Walsingham along the track of an old railway to reach the pretty hamlet of Houghton St Giles, on the edge of which stands the 14th-century Slipper Chapel, the Roman Catholic shrine (said to be where pilgrims including Henry VIII removed their shoes to walk barefoot into Walsingham). A huge modern church stands next to it. The parish church of St Giles has a 15th-century rood screen. Next the walk follows a track uphill towards the site of the medieval village of Egmere, where ruined St Edmund's church now stands forlorn. This hill is one of the

highest in Norfolk and affords excellent views back over Walsingham and the valley of the little river Stiffkey. The return to Walsingham passes the light railway which takes passengers via Wighton and Warham to Wells-next-the-Sea.

THE WALK

❶ Leave via the entrance the other side of the car park from the big mill building and turn left along narrow Coker's Hill, full of interesting cottages. Cross over Station Road, which on the right leads to the old station, now a Greek Orthodox church, and carry on, passing the ruins of the friary built into a later house.

❷ Where the lane bears round to the left, turn right up a short stretch of track which comes to a wide grassy space – the track of an old railway. Turn left along this and continue out into rolling countryside until the Slipper Chapel and barn-like modern church next to it near the hamlet of Houghton St Giles come into view.

PLACES of INTEREST

Wells and Walsingham Light Railway with stops at Warham and Wighton (telephone: 01328 856506. The grounds of **Walsingham Abbey**, which include the 12th-century Augustinian priory ruins and the great arch of the east window of the church, are privately owned but can be visited at certain times, especially rewarding in the snowdrop season (telephone: 01328 820259). **Shirehall Museum** (telephone: 01328 820510). For guided tours of Walsingham telephone: 01328 820250. At Great Walsingham there is the **Textile Centre** with displays of screen printing and hand printing fabrics, shop and coffee shop (telephone: 01328 820900). **Pensthorpe Waterfowl Park** near Fakenham (telephone: 01328 851465).

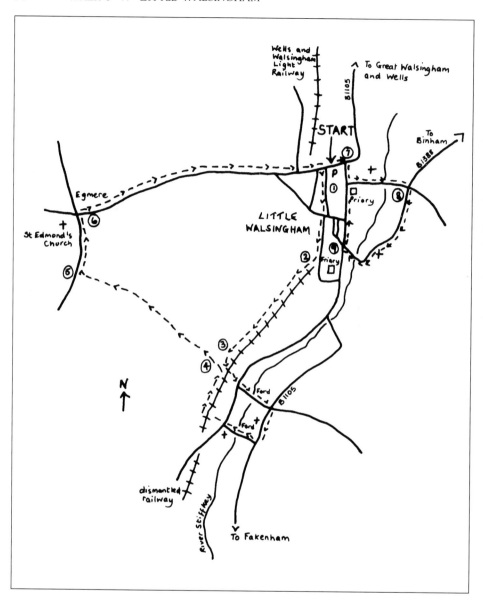

❸ Go down steps to the right of a wooden barrier by a broken railway bridge, and turn left down the unmade-up lane to reach a small road. Turn right for a short distance then take a left turn signposted to Houghton St Giles which leads over a footbridge next to a ford over the little river Stiffkey. At the crossroads turn right, signposted to Fakenham. Pass the church of St Giles with a red brick Victorian

Common Place, with its 16th-century pump house.

former rectory behind. Just beyond the church take a small lane to the right over another footbridge next to a ford to the Slipper Chapel complex. Cross a lane and go for a short distance up a track to steps up to the disused railway again, turning right to return along it for a short distance to the broken bridge.

❹ Leave the track of the old railway to turn left up a broad sandy track which runs for over a mile uphill between hedges studded with the odd tree. About halfway the track passes a house with a lovely old barn next to it.

❺ At the road, turn right and walk towards the line of houses which is now the hamlet of Egmere.

❻ At the next crossroads turn right (signposted to Walsingham) down a narrow lane with passing places. Carry on for about 1½ miles, ignoring side roads and passing the terminus of the Wells to Walsingham Railway on the left. Continue on down, passing Coker's Hill on the right which leads back to the car park. The road ahead becomes Guild Street (note Guild House) at the bottom of which a right turn passes the 16th-century half-timbered Refectory of the College of Clergy.

❼ For this walk, turn right opposite the Robin Hood inn, along Bridewell Street (the name comes from the old prison still with treadmills which stands nearby), which is full of interesting cottages, houses and alleys. Notice King's House (1632) with its bust of King Charles. After

Common Place with the pump building in the middle, the timbered Shrine Shop on the left, and the Shirehall Museum and tourist office on the far side, bear left to go down Holt Road with the picturesque Bull Inn on the right, following along the high flint walls of the abbey grounds. Pass the Shrine of Our Lady of Walsingham in peaceful grounds on the left. Cross over Knight Street which goes to the left and continue on along the pavement, noting the old milestone in front of the abbey walls.

❽ At the next crossroads turn right along Sunk Road which bisects the abbey grounds, eventually passing the church of St Mary on the left which burnt down and was rebuilt in 1961. The road bends to the right and becomes Church Street, crossing the river Stiffkey.

❾ At the junction with the B1105 to Fakenham, turn right to go up the High Street, pausing to slip left for a few minutes into Friday Market to see the Methodist chapel of 1794, the old grammar school, now the Pilgrim's Bureau, and the 15th-century Black Lion Hotel on the corner. Return to the High Street which is a fascinating hotchpotch of old and interesting buildings, many housing places of refreshment. Pass Almonry Lane on the left and further on a little arch through to Swan Entry. An ancient gateway on the right leads into the abbey grounds. Turn left to get back to the car park from Common Place.

LETHERINGSETT

Length: 2 miles

Getting There: Letheringsett is on the junction of the A148 between Fakenham and Cromer with the B1156 from Blakeney.

Parking: Down the lane near the church.

Map: OS Landranger 133 North East Norfolk (GR 060390).

Despite its small size, Letheringsett is packed with interest and the surrounding countryside in the valley of the river Glaven is particularly beautiful. The local estate was revamped by owner William Hardy who left his mark on the lovely old brewery buildings as well as on the road bridge of 1818 and the Doric colonnade fronting Letheringsett Hall. The walk passes these and goes on to Letheringsett watermill, rebuilt in 1757 in the Tuscan style and again in 1802 for the Lether-

ingsett Hall estate. It was restored by an estate worker in 1982 and now produces and sells wholemeal stone ground flour and associated products. The church of St Andrew with its 11th-century round tower is equally interesting. It was restored in the late 19th century by William Butterfield and excellent stained glass by Charles Kempe was added. A tombstone near the gate to the churchyard records the death of Jason Jex, a notable local blacksmith and watchmaker, whose death mask is in

---

FOOD and DRINK

The King's Head, set in a large garden, is an excellent freehouse serving well kept real ales and a range of malts as well as interesting bar food. Telephone: 01263 712691.

---

river Glaven runs over a ford on the outskirts of the village and a path runs alongside it through water meadows which can be used to extend the walk. The wildflowers along the route of this walk are particularly good.

the church and to whom is attributed the clock on the old brewery buildings.

There are some very attractive cottages along the route of the walk as well as interesting converted barns. The pretty

THE WALK

❶ From the church cross the busy A148 road carefully and walk to the left along the pavement. Pass the King's Head pub off the main road to the right. Just by the lane to the King's Head are splendid estate

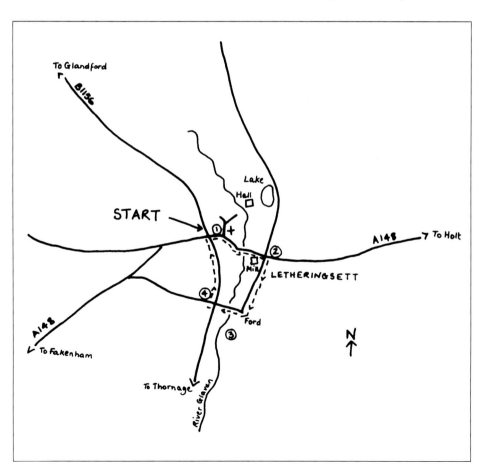

The church of St Andrew.

and former brewery buildings marked with 'WH 1814'. 'WH' refers to William Hardy who built up various parts of his estate around that date and added a Doric colonnade to Letheringsett Hall. The building further on houses a chiming clock and has an oast chimney on its roof. Cross the famous bridge over river Glaven, dated 1818 and 'erected by subscription under the plan and direction of WH'. Continue along the road, passing a pretty row of terraced cottages on the left and an old red phone box on the right with a splendid flint wall behind. Garden Lane goes off on the left leading to Letheringsett Lake where day tickets are available for coarse fishing. Also down this lane are various footpath markers for permissive walks on the lovely Bayfield estate.

❷ Turn right by a grassy triangle to Letheringsett watermill along Riverside Road, a peaceful contrast to the A148. Continue on past more splendid farm buildings, partially converted, and some pretty brick and cut flint cottages with gothic windows and plaques with the estate's coat of arms. Further on from the Primitive Methodist church of 1898 on the right, the lane leads out into the countryside, passing more converted barns to reach a ford. Just ahead are water meadows in the Countryside Stewardship scheme

---

PLACES of INTEREST

Letheringsett watermill (telephone: 01263 713153). **Natural Surroundings wildflower centre**, Bayford, (telephone 01263 711091). **Glandford Shell Museum**. Walks in the conifer woods and heathland of **Holt Lowes Country Park**, to the south of Holt. **Baconsthorpe Castle** (English Heritage) moated and mostly ruined 15th-century fortified house, reached from the A148 at Holt.

which offers walks along the river through flowery meadows.

❸ This walk turns right over a bridge over by the ford and continues on, passing con-verted stables and more pretty cottages to a small crossroads.

❹ Turn right here in Little Thornage along the road signposted to Glandford and Blakeney. This quiet lane, hedged on both sides, leads gently back uphill between banks of wildflowers with an occasional house. The road south leads to Thornage where the Bishops of Norwich had a summer mansion. At the junction with the main A148 road, the lane oppo-site leads to Bayfield Hall and estate with more permissive walks. Turn right back to St Andrew's church with its former rectory opposite made of pebbles with brick facings. Further down the lane is Lether-ingsett Hall, now an old people's home.

OVERSTRAND

Length: 5 miles

Getting there: Overstrand is about 2 miles from Cromer on the B1159 to Mundesley.	**Parking:** Pay and display cliff top park (with toilets) at the end of Paul's Lane, signposted from the B1159.	**Map:** OS Landranger 133 North East Norfolk (GR 246410).

Poppyland – the very name conjures up images of Edwardian romanticism – an appreciation of natural beauty and exciting scenery combined with a solid desire for warmth and comfort that only money can bring. Overstrand, originally a humble fishing village, became popular with the rich and famous during Edwardian times following poet and writer Clement Scott's lyrical newspaper articles about the area. The village still retains something of the atmosphere of that time – a feeling of the

arts and crafts movement, and of garden cities. Some of the big houses, built for rich and titled people by famous architects of the time such as Lutyens and Bloomfield, are still visible even if their function has changed. The Pleasaunce (1897) was designed by Lutyens with gardens by Gertrude Jekyll for Lord Battersea, Chief Whip in Gladstone's cabinet, whose wife was a Rothschild. Lutyens also designed Overstrand Hall (1899) for Lord Hillingdon, a London banker, and the Methodist

FOOD and DRINK

The Parson's Pleasure in Northrepps, a friendly pub, restaurant and hotel in a beautifully converted old barn (telephone: 01263 579691). Also in Northrepps is the Foundry Arms pub which does morning coffee and inexpensive food (telephone 01263 579256). Northrepps Cottage restaurant and carvery – which also offers bed and breakfast – is passed on the walk (telephone: 01263 513178). In Overstrand you will find the Cliff Top Café and hotels which include Seamarge (advertising cream teas) and the Overstrand Court Hotel opposite. There is also the Poppyland tearoom in the Overstrand Cottage Garden Centre on the Mundesley road (telephone: 01263 579485).

chapel. Mock Tudor Seamarge, built by Arthur Bloomfield in 1908, had impressive Italianate gardens. Even Winston Churchill's father owned a house in the village (Pear Tree Cottage). This walk explores the remnants of gentility in Overstrand, perched on its crumbling cliffs.

Leaving Overstrand, the walk climbs uphill along narrow lanes hung with trees or edged with flowery banks emblazoned with summertime poppies – the essence of the area made famous by Clement Scott as Poppyland. At the top of the hill, the interesting small village of Northrepps was once the home (Northrepps Hall) of Sir Thomas Fowell-Buxton who helped William Wilberforce to abolish slavery. The Foundry Arms pub is a reminder of the nearby foundry where the Gallas plough was developed. The business no longer functions but the forges, furnaces, castingboxes and 19th-century engines are still intact. Returning down the hill to Overstrand, the walk finishes near the beach where the cliffs are revealing fossils

and semi-precious stones – agate, cornelian, jet and amber.

THE WALK

❶ From the car park walk up Paul's Lane, away from the sea, with glimpses of former architectural glories such as the coach house with an old clock face on the left. Pass a side road to Hillingdon Park and then splendid 'arts and crafts' Danum House, once home of the Edwardian novelist Florence Barclay, on the corner. Just here a footpath bears off to the right through railings to St Martin's church. In the 14th century the old church fell into the sea and this new one was built, incorporating the ruins of a medieval church. Inside are several tombs and memorials including one to Anna Gurney who with her friend Sarah Buxton founded The Belfry School on the main road early in the 19th century.

❷ Turn right along the main road and then, almost opposite the drive to Overstrand Hall, turn left up Northrepps Road. The road soon passes through lovely mixed woodland with a wealth of rhododendrons. Turn left down a narrow lane near the Northrepps Cottage restaurant complex. Follow the lane as it bends to the right, going gently uphill. At a road junc-

PLACES of INTEREST

Felbrigg Hall (National Trust, telephone: 01263 837444) is to the south-west. The North Norfolk Railway (the Poppy line), running between Sheringham and Holt (telephone: 01263 822045). Cromer Museum has a display connected with Poppyland (telephone: 01263 513543).

The delightful east window in St Martin's church.

tion ignore the right turn and go straight ahead, enjoying the excellent views.

❸ Turn right off the road onto a broad signposted track and almost immediately bear left off the track along a narrow signposted path alongside a hedged bank on the right. Cross a metalled lane and carry on along a broad green lane running between hedges. The lane narrows; ignore a stile into a field by the church on the left and continue on, passing a deep tree-grown pit on the left to come out into a meadow. Ignore the gate on the right and follow the path veering to right and left all the way round to a double gate with a stile to the right. Then follow the hedge on the left. Ignore a stile on the left into a rough field and keep on along a fence towards the church. Go through a gap into the churchyard of 11th-century St Mary's, Northrepps. Leave the churchyard

through smart memorial gates and turn left into Northrepps village, passing the former rectory and then the Parson's Pleasure hotel/pub. The road bears to the right and reaches a junction. Further on to the right is the Foundry Arms pub.

❹ Bear left to the junction by the village sign, cross and take the lane to the right (Church Street leading to Bull's Row). Cross over a side turn to Broadgate Close and, where the road bears right, take a metalled lane to the left. After two houses, the lane becomes green underfoot and passes between scrappy hedgerows. As the woods on the left approach the track, leave it and slip to the right of it along a narrow signposted track which runs downhill beneath a tunnel of trees. Go through a metal barrier and continue on. At a T junction of tracks near allotments, bear left along a broad track which curves

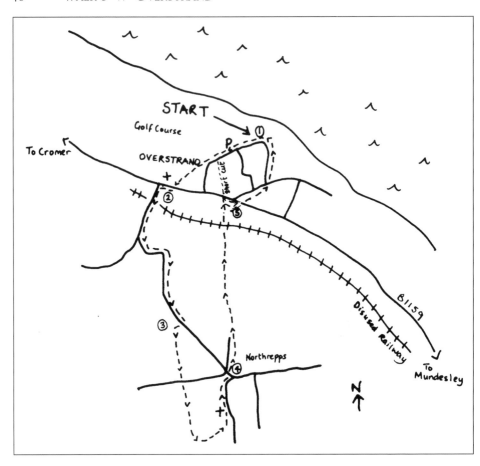

rightish, going over an old railway track to come out onto the main road via a broad gravelled area.

❺ For a short cut, cross over and continue on along a narrow path through a metal barrier, turning right along the road back to the car park.

For the main walk, turn right along the main road for a short distance, then bear left along High Street. Just by the well hedged sports club, look left down Harbord Road to see the many pillared wrought iron entrance gates to The Pleasaunce, then carry on, passing shops and a pretty post office with wrought iron pillars. Turn left down Cliff Road, passing the Methodist chapel, to come out on the cliff top near the old fishing settlement of Beckhythe, now crumbled into the sea. Turn left back to the car park, passing the grounds of The Pleasaunce, now a Christian holiday centre. To see Seamarge continue on before turning down Cliff Road. Near the car park steps go down to the sandy beach which is covered at very high tides.

MELTON CONSTABLE
Length: 4½ miles

Getting there: Melton Constable is halfway between Fakenham and Aylsham on the B1354.	Parking: There is a layby by the Melton Constable sign on the B1354 at the Fakenham end of the village	Map: OS Landranger 133 North East Norfolk (GR 041331).

Melton Constable is unlike any other village in Norfolk. Reminiscent of the terraced villages of the industrial north, it came into being because the local lord of the manor, Lord Hastings, decided to drag rural Norfolk into the age of the locomotive and built the junction and locomotive works of the Midland and Great Northern Railway on his land. Dubbed the Muddle and Get Nowhere line, it opened in 1887 and closed in 1964, leaving various interesting chunks of industrial archaeology.

Marriott Way, leading to the site, is named after the chief engineer of the line who had an ornate villa in the village and wrote the history of the line in *Forty Years of a Norfolk Railway*. He also gave his name to a walking and riding route using part of the old line which linked Norwich and King's Lynn.

There is a huge contrast in this walk between the industrial nature of the village and the remote countryside around. Another contrast is between the tight ter-

FOOD and DRINK

The Hunny Belle in Hunworth is excellent for families (telephone: 01263 861383). The John H Stracey in Briston has an excellent restaurant, and also offers bar meals (telephone: 01263 860891).

races in the village and the beautiful late 17th-century hall of the railway owner, set a careful distance away surrounded by lovely parkland landscaped by Capability Brown in 1764–9. The estate was owned by the Astley family from 1236 until this century. It was the Victorian Astley, Lord Hastings, who founded the railway. Glimpses of the house can be seen from the interesting church of St Peter in the park with its early Norman central tower. Inside are notable Astley memorials and the lavish Astley family pew.

THE WALK

❶ Walk into the village, passing the former Railway Hotel and the late Victorian railway workers' institute. A violin maker's workshop has taken over a little railway building. The main village street consists of late Victorian and Edwardian terraces. Go over two side turns, Gordon Road and Kitchener Road (with more brick terraces).

❷ Turn left along Burgh Beck Road at the end of which is a signposted broad track bending to the right then left to a metal gate. Slip to the right here towards a stable complex but bear immediately left again to go along a narrow track between fencing on the right and the hedge of the gated green lane on the left. Passing a pond on the right, bear right at the corner between fences and then left over a stile at the bottom (arrow marked). Continue straight

The village church.

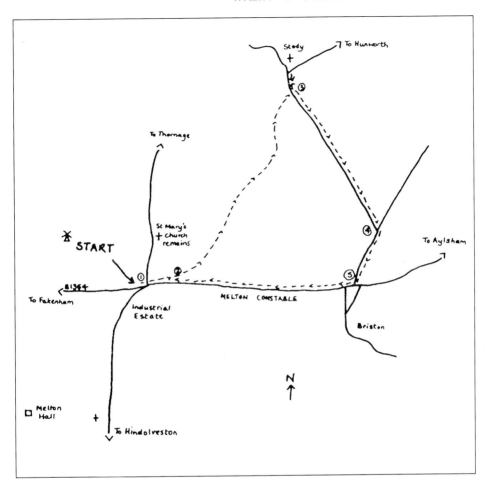

ahead across a rough field towards some bushes where there is an arrow marked post on the right. Cross another stile (arrow marked) and continue on into a field. Skirt to the right, following the field boundary, with glimpses on the left of the ruined tower of St Mary's church and a mill high up on the slope beyond. A stream is almost hidden on the right. Go through by a broken stile (arrow marked), cross a little bridge and continue on along the edge of another field. Cross the stream

via an arrow marked wooden bridge and continue on ahead along the edge of another field with a hedgerow on the left. At the end of the field go through a rough area, bearing slightly to the right and then

---

PLACES of INTEREST

The Thursford Collection of organs and steam machines (telephone: 01328 878477). This can be reached along the B1354 to the west.

over a stile by a metal gate (arrow marked). Go straight over the field but at the opposite corner ignore a metal gate on the right and turn left down the edge of the field, then right and left all the way round the edge to a stile by double metal gates near a wood (the alternative would be to go diagonally across the field). Cross the stile, bear left along a broad track to another stile by a gate. Cross this and go straight on through a meadow along a track alongside a wood then a fence and hedge towards the pretty hamlet of Stody. Cross the stile by a metal gate onto the road and turn left to visit Stody and its ancient church brooding over an undulating valley. Just before the church a lane to the right and then another right turn lead to the pretty village of Hunworth with a pleasant pub (the Hunny Belle) on the edge of a lovely green.

❸ For the main walk, ignore this and return down the road away from Stody. The high banked lane flattens out and skirts a large wood, passing pretty thatched lodges, and comes eventually to a cross-roads.

❹ Turn right along a more major road (Horseshoe Common), signposted to Briston and Thurning, and reach the main road. The John H Stracey pub is further to the left.

❺ To continue the main walk, cross Fakenham Road and walk to the right along the pavement. Ignore all side turnings. There is scattered housing, a school and then a tract of open countryside before the start of Melton Constable. Continue over various side streets to Marriott Way on the left. This leads to the industrial area where the workshop and sidings of the railway were. Industrial archaeology enthusiasts will find many traces of former railway buildings. Continue on back to the parking area. Just further on, the left turn signposted to Hindolveston and Foulsham leads to Melton Hall and its church.

ALDBOROUGH
Length: 5 miles

Getting There: Aldborough is about 5 miles north of Aylsham to the west of the A140 Aylsham to Cromer road.

Parking: Near the village green.

Map: OS Landranger 133 North East Norfolk (GR 185343).

This small north Norfolk village is set in the heart of prime farming country with a network of waterways providing excellent irrigation. Its chief glory is its large triangular village green, big enough for a cricket pitch, bordered by lovely houses, some dating back to the 17th and early 18th centuries, and a smattering of shops and pubs. The churches in this region seem to be at some distance from the villages and St Mary's, with the notable Old Rectory, is about ½ mile west of Aldborough, with the

Hall (16th century with later additions) another mile north-west. The church is worth a visit for its memorial brasses and for the spring flowers in the churchyard – a legacy from a Victorian rector who was a bulb specialist.

The walk meanders through gentle pastoral scenery with excellent views from such vantage points as delightful Thwaite church, set on a ridge, with a round tower, a canopied Jacobean pulpit and a Victorian schoolroom on the north side. Down

FOOD and DRINK

In Aldborough the Black Boys pub (late 17th century) offers good food and bar snacks (telephone: 01263 768086) and the Old Red Lion is a Georgian village restaurant with bar snacks and à la carte menu (telephone: 01263 761451). The Spread Eagle in Erpingham specialises in Woodforde's ales which used to be brewed in the barn next to the pub until it had to move to larger premises at Woodbastwick (telephone: 01263 761591).

in the valley, the walk crosses wild Thwaite Common to reach the village of Erpingham which also has a solitary church, set ½ mile to the south. The lofty 15th-century tower of St Mary's church has ERPYNGHM spelt out in stone round the parapet and was supposedly erected by lord of the manor Sir Thomas Erpingham, a famous warrior, who accompanied Henry V at the Battle of Agincourt and had the Erpingham Gate (1420) into Norwich Cathedral Close named after him. Inside is a splendid brass memorial to his father, Sir John. The walk then continues through fields, passing picturesque Aldborough mill to return to the village green. Part of the walk follows the Weavers' Way (a 56 mile walking route between Cromer and Great Yarmouth).

THE WALK

❶ Walk past the Old Red Lion to the junction, with the Community Centre on the left. Ignore the left-hand road going alongside the green and continue on down a small lane lined with a mixture of dwellings. Cross over a stream and follow the bends of the lane, passing a Methodist chapel of 1907. Look for a path to the right

just before another bend, which crosses a wooden bridge and stile (arrow marked). Walk through the meadow here, going through posts by a wet area to cross a stile onto another lane. Turn right here, cross a white railinged bridge and follow this leafy lane round, passing Aldborough primary school on the left.

❷ At the next junction, before the houses of Alby Hill, turn right along another lane, then very shortly cross a stile to the left onto a footpath (signposted Weavers' Way) along the edge of a meadow with a farm beyond the boundary on the left. Cross into another field (arrow marker). At the corner of the field go to the right, then left at the end of a strip of woodland. Carry straight on down the next section of field to go through metal gates onto a road. Round towered Thwaite All Saints' church is on the left and several other churches punctuate the lovely view, including St Mary's, Erpingham directly ahead and the squat towered church of Our Lady and St Margaret at Calthorpe more to the right.

For a short cut, you could turn right here and then take the next right turn, picking up the main walk again and following the directions from point ❻.

❸ For the main walk, turn left at the road, then very quickly right down a marked

PLACES of INTEREST

Mannington Gardens and **Wolterton Hall Gardens** (telephone: 01263 584175) to the south-west of Aldborough. **Alby Craft Centre** – with tearoom – at Alby (telephone: 01263 768719).

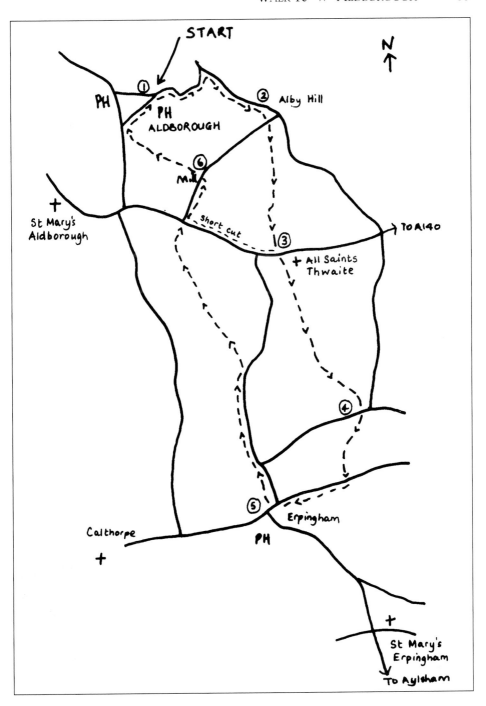

All Saints' church, Thwaite.

path by the side of the church along the edge of a field. Bear left and right round the edge of the field, then go along a baulk between fields. Continue on over a farm track and go up the next field, baulk. A marker on a post points the path slightly to the left through crops to come out on a lane near a red brick house.

❹ Turn right, ignoring another turn to the left. Where the lane bends sharply to the right, bear left over Thwaite Common, following the marked path. Cross a two-step stile and go ahead, following the line of the fence on the left. Veer away from the fence shortly and bear slightly to the right along a path through the middle of the common to an arrow marked gate. Cross a footbridge over a stream and continue on along a narrow fenced off path. Cross a stile and follow the footpath onto a road. Turn right into Erpingham, passing the village hall. Continue on through a mixture of houses to a right turn (Chapel Road). For the Spread Eagle pub, continue straight on to the next junction.

❺ To continue the walk, turn right along Chapel Road, passing the chapel. Ignore a turn to the right alongside Thwaite Common and, soon after a section of woodland, turn left off the road down a signposted broad track. Go over a wooden bridge and through metal gates. The fenced track curves left to Meadow Cottage. At this point look for a stile on the right, cross this and go straight ahead through a field towards a hedgerow where a step stile leads up into the next field. Continue straight over to a wooden footpath signpost. Go down the bank, cross a road and go ahead down the little lane opposite.

❻ Where the lane bends to the right, turn left and go along a signposted path (Weavers' Way) by a fence and hedge. Continue on, passing Aldborough water-mill on the left. Cross a bridge and go down a shady path between houses and come out onto a gravelled area in front of the mill. Bear rightish down the lane, passing through an arrow marked wooden gate, and meet the road by a garage. Turn right down the road back into the village of Aldborough.

WORSTEAD

Length: 4½ miles

Getting there: Worstead is down a turning off the A149 a few miles south of North Walsham.	Parking: Near the church in Church Plain or in the Weavers' Way car park just north-east of Briggate.	Map: OS Landranger 133 North East Norfolk or 134 Norwich and The Broads (GR 302260).

The elegant and substantial houses of today's Worstead bear testimony to past greatness and prosperity founded on sheep rearing and weaving in the Middle Ages, when the village gave its name to a special type of cloth. The great church of St Mary, which is still home to a present-day Guild of Weavers, Spinners and Dyers, with a display in one of the aisles, is a lasting result of that prosperity (note the beautifully carved and painted rood screen of 1512). Flemish weavers had settled in the area and brought special skills with them. The village fell into a decline as the

FOOD and DRINK

The New Inn (1825) with a pleasant beer garden does morning coffee and bar snacks. It has a touring caravan site and also offers bed and breakfast (telephone: 01692 536296).

cottage industry shrank, finished off eventually by the Industrial Revolution when trade moved to the big mills of the north. Some of the houses on Church Plain date back to the early 17th century. The elegant Manor House is opposite the church and on the other corner is an interesting building called Geoffrey the Dyer's House (named after the man who led the local Peasants' Revolt), which seems to have been a merchant's house converted later to a row of weavers' cottages. Further round the square is St Andrew's Cottage with steps at the front leading down to a smugglers' tunnel linked with long gone St Andrew's church. In its heyday, Worstead would have been much longer with access through medieval gates – Withergate, Bengate, Briggate and Lyngate which are now small hamlets outside the village.

As well as visiting these pretty outposts, the walk takes in part of the Weavers' Way (a long distance footpath running between Cromer and Great Yarmouth) which here passes along the track of an old railway. It crosses the disused North Walsham and Dilham Canal opened in 1825 and running for nine miles to connect North Walsham with the river Ant and the Broads waterways. It is now a pretty backwater, host to all kinds of plant, bird and insect life. Nearby Briggate mill, now a ruin, was one of the largest mills in Britain.

THE WALK

❶ From the central square of Church Plain walk between the church on the left and the Manor House on the right in a westerly direction. Just before the Worstead sign, turn right up a small lane, following the wall of the Manor House grounds and passing farm buildings on the right, then the burial ground and the new and old rectories on the left. Ignore a lane going back into the village on the right and bear left, continuing out into the country.

❷ Just before the cottages of Withergate, take a signed path to the right over a little wooden bridge and then a stile (arrow marked). Go ahead along the edge of an open field with trees and hedge to the left. Pass a large pond seen through a gate on the left and at the end of the field cross a stile (arrow marked), bear left and go through a gap in the hedge (arrow mark on post) over a ditch then right down the edge of the field. Turn left along the hedge and then right at the hedge corner (another arrow marker) and carry on along a stony track, passing between a bungalow and a cottage. This bears to the right between the houses of Bengate to a lane.

For a short cut, follow the lane right, turning right and then left at T junctions back to the village.

PLACES of INTEREST

Beeston Hall and gardens (telephone: 01692 630711) is to the south, reached from the A1151 Norwich road. In **Sutton**, along the A149 to the south-east of Worstead, you can visit the windmill and museum of bygones (telephone: 01692 581195).

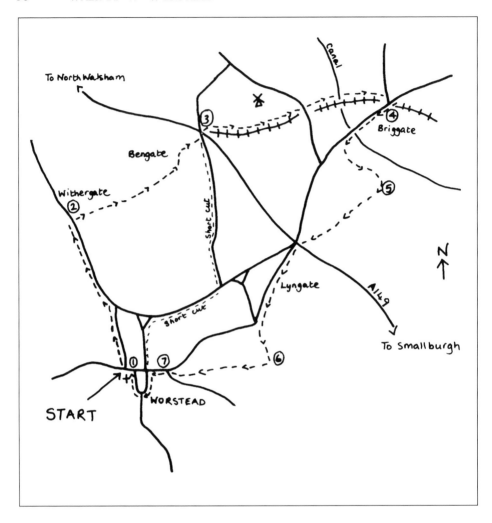

❸ For the main walk, follow the lane to the left through a tunnel under the A149 to come out near a dismantled railway line (once part of the Midland and Great Northern or Muddle and Get Nowhere line), now part of the Weavers' Way (noticeboard and arrow markers). Turn right through the open gate and go up steps onto the old railway embankment. Carry on to where the path goes through by a gate and across a little lane leading to Briggate. Pass The Gatehouse on the left and continue on through a gate on the other side. Further on the path crosses the disused North Walsham and Dilham Canal via two wooden footbridges and comes out into a grassy clearing with a seat. At the end of this (marker post) bear right off the Weavers' Way through a car park.

The path back to the village.

❹ Bear right to the road, turning right into Briggate. Cross over the canal again on a road bridge with the remains of Briggate mill on the left. Turn left down White Horse Lane which wiggles round, passing cottages to reach open country.

❺ Turn right up a wide green lane just before Briggate Farm and head back towards Worstead in line with the church tower through open fields. Cross the busy A149, bearing slightly to the right, and walk down the lane opposite, signposted to Worstead. Very shortly, turn left down Barnard's Road in the hamlet of Lyngate. At a T junction bear left and when the road bends to the right keep straight on ahead along a broad stony track (footpath signpost).

❻ Just past Dairyhouse barn on the left, turn right at a signpost along a footpath through a field towards the church. Come out onto the road, ignore the turn to the right and continue ahead down Honing Row back to the centre of the village, passing an assortment of interesting buildings including a converted chapel of 1892.

❼ Turn left into Church Plain, continue past the church and down Front Street, passing the New Inn and a pretty mix of old cottages. Bear left at the road junction to walk back to the main square, passing the post office on the left.

WALK 12

WINTERTON
Length: 5 miles

Getting there: Winterton is about 6 miles north of Great Yarmouth on the B1159.

Parking: On King's Corner to the right of the main road (Beach Road) outside the Winterton Youth and Community Centre (free) or the beach car park (paying) with toilets nearby.

Map: OS Landranger 134 Norwich and The Broads (GR 495196).

Once just a winter camp for fisherman, Winterton had become a permanent village by the time of the Norman Conquest. It is not a picture postcard village but a cosy jumble of cottages and houses in an attractive mixture of building materials – brick, flint, pebble, or colour washed with roofs of thatch, slate or pantiles. Small alleys called lokes run from the main streets. The huge 132 ft tower of the church of the Holy Trinity and All Saints was a landmark for sailors who ran the risk of shipwreck on Winterton Ness a little further up the coast. Here towards the

FOOD and DRINK

The 300 year old Fisherman's Return pub has a wide variety of real ales plus an excellent menu including constantly changing specials such as moules marinière and local fish. A separate garden room and enclosed garden are good for families. Bed and breakfast is also available (telephone: 01493 393305). The Beach Cafe near the coastguard lookout is open seasonally.

THE WALK

❶ From the parking area turn left and walk along Beach Road away from the sea, ignoring all turnings to right and left. Pass the post office and further on, on the left, the Primitive Methodist chapel of 1876. On the right leading from Market Place is North Market Road where the public footpath through the nature reserve comes out. Then to the left is The Lane leading to the Fisherman's Return pub. Continue along the main road, now called Black Street, passing the beautifully carved and painted Winterton sign on a green. After the school with its decorative brickwork you come to the 12th-century church with its early 15th-century tower of knapped flint embellished with gargoyles and figures. At the end of the churchyard, turn immediately right along a broad track leading past allotments.

end of the 17th century two hundred ships and more than a thousand men were lost in a dreadful storm. The lighthouse on a ridge behind the beach ceased functioning in 1921. From Wolly Bolly, one of the giant sandhills near the dunes, you can have an overview of Winterton's great assets – its magnificent sandy, shelving beach and its acid dune nature reserve run by English Nature which blazes with heathers in August and September and rhododendrons in spring.

   Part of this walk follows the Winterton Parish Walk going towards East and West Somerton and passing the ruins of St Mary's church and elegant Burnley Hall. Not far from here is the church of St Mary the Virgin, West Somerton, with the tomb of the Norfolk giant in the churchyard. Turning north through attractive shooting coverts where dogs must be firmly on leads, the walk then reaches the nature reserve near Winterton Ness where there is a choice of walking back to Winterton through the reserve, often among amazing clouds of butterflies and dragonflies, or along the lovely shelving sandy beach protected by groynes. The restless white sails of a wind farm are a constant background to the walk.

❷ At a T junction of tracks turn left, passing Low Farm on the left to reach a lane at a corner. Go ahead and then follow the bends of the road as it passes the lovely old buildings and pond of Manor Farm on the left. At a junction carry straight on along Low Road, ignoring the turn to the left. Pheasants scuttle through the ruins of old St Mary's church on the left, almost hidden in trees. Continue on along the

PLACES of INTEREST

Great Yarmouth offers many attractions (Tourist Office telephone: 01493 842195). **Horsey and Hickling Broads** to the north-west of Winterton. **Thrigby Hall Wildlife Garden** to the south-west, off the A1064 (telephone: 01493 369477).

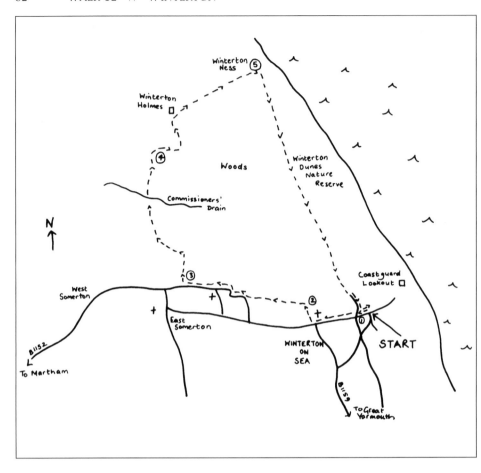

concrete road without turning off, passing the interesting complex of buildings associated with Queen Anne Burnley Hall.

❸ At a T junction leading to a lane, take a concreted track to the right to follow the main walk.

For those interested in giants follow the lane bearing round to the left, joining the main road for a short distance to reach the church of St Mary the Virgin, West Somerton, with its round Norman tower. In the churchyard stands the tomb of Robert Hales, the Norfolk giant, who was born in the village in the early 19th century and grew to 7ft 8in tall. To continue the walk, retrace your steps and turn left.

Continue along the concrete lane (arrow marker on post) passing a pretty gamekeeper's cottage. Pass a thatched cottage and bear left at the corner. Bear right at the next corner, continuing along the concrete track (Holmes Road) through a pleasant avenue of willows with a view of Horsey windmill complete with sails over the field ahead. Cross over Commission-

The village pub.

ers' Drain and go out into more open grazing marshes.

❹ Where the concrete road goes straight on, turn right (signposted) along a broad stony path left at the field edge. Turn left towards the orange roof of a barn and then turn sharp right to reach it (footpath signpost). Cross the hard standing and continue straight on at a crossroad of tracks (arrow marker post) and continue on along a broad stony track towards the dunes, passing through a pretty wooded area of silver birch and oak. Go through to the left of a gate onto the reserve itself. An English Nature notice board by concrete blocks warns of adders. The Winterton Dunes National Nature Reserve is part of the largest dune system in East Anglia and is important for sea defences as well as being of geological interest. Little terns nest on the beach from May to July and common and grey seals have their pups here.

❺ There is a choice of route either through the reserve, following the signposted route to the right, or along the beach. From the high dunes by the beach you can see back to Winterton and the old lighthouse on a hill by the village or in the other direction to red striped Happisburgh lighthouse and various churches. After about a mile along the beach look for a gap in the dunes near the coastguard lookout and turn right to meet the beach road leading back to the village.

LUDHAM

Length: 6¼ miles

Getting there: Ludham is on the A1062 about 2 miles west of Potter Heigham.	Parking: In Stocks Hill outside St Catherine's church or near the King's Arms pub. Free parking at How Hill, on the route of the walk.	Map: OS Landranger 133 North East Norfolk or 134 Norwich and The Broads (GR 389184).

This picturesque Broadland village has been linked to nearby St Benet's Abbey since King Canute gave the local manor to the monks in 1019. Being almost surrounded by water with the river Ant to the west, the river Bure joining the Thurne to the south and Womack Water to the south-east, it is no wonder that Ludham's fortunes have been linked to its waterways. Mills abound – windmills for grinding local corn and watermills for draining the marshes and maintaining the waterways. The wherry trade brought rich merchants who spent their money on fine houses in the village. Pretty cottages once housed a host of different trades, most now gone

FOOD and DRINK

The King's Arms opposite the church is open every day for bar food and all day at weekends (telephone: 01692 678386). Next door is Alfresco in a pretty listed thatched cottage which does excellent morning coffee, lunches and afternoon teas (dinner is by booking only) but is closed on Mondays and for two weeks in early November and most of January and February (telephone: 01692 678384). About a mile out of the village is the Dog Inn at Ludham Bridge, popular with the boating fraternity (telephone: 01692 630321).

though boat building still goes on at Womack Water. St Catherine's church is 15th century with an earlier chancel. Inside, painted saints decorate a fine late 15th-century screen, while some of the carvings on the 15th-century font are linked with pagan times.

The walk passes along tracks and tiny lanes towards the woods and wetlands near beautiful thatched How Hill house with its renowned azalea garden dominating the banks of the river Ant. Here, near the staithe where reed and sedge are landed, stands Toad Hole, a renovated marshman's cottage and museum. Nearby are three drainage mills of different designs. The walk continues on to pass Ludham Hall, its Georgian front masking a Jacobean building, with an adjoining 17th-century chapel now used as a barn. This was once a country house for the Bishops of Norwich. A footpath (an extension to the main walk) leads south to St Benet's Abbey, now romantic ruins with the remains of a windmill rising out of them. Everywhere are wonderful views over typical Broadland scenery graced with the occasional sail wafting through the countryside.

THE WALK

❶ From the central square walk east away from the King's Arms along Yarmouth Road, passing the village sign on Baker's Arms Green recalling a former pub which had a bakery attached in Victorian times. Go through metal railings on the right-hand side of the road along a footpath away from the traffic. Come out onto the road near a pleasant green where a detour to the right leads down Horsefen Road to Womack Staithe where the famous wherry, the *Albion*, is moored.

❷ To continue the walk, carry on along the main road, then just beyond the turn into Latchmore Park, turn left into Latchmore Lane (signposted 'Byroad'). Soon at a T junction of lanes bear right and wind along to a crossroads of lanes where you turn left at Malthouse Farmhouse.

❸ Carry on to another T junction and turn right, signposted to Catfield.

❹ Almost opposite a cottage, turn left along a green lane through fields. Cross a minor road and continue (waymarked) along a narrow path passing between fields.

❺ At a cross track (waymark post), turn

PLACES of INTEREST

Fairhaven Garden Trust (telephone: 01603 270683) to the south at South Walsham. **Hoveton Hall Garden** and **Wroxham Barns Craft Centre** (telephone: 01603 783762), both to the west of Ludham and reached off the A1062. **Fleggburgh Bygone Village** (telephone: 01493 369770), reached from the B1152 south of Potter Heigham.

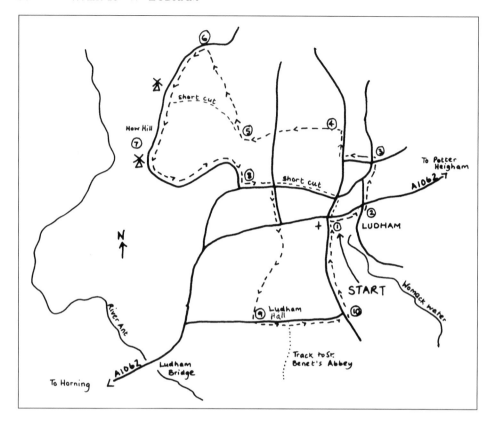

right along a wide grassy path, ignoring the footpath to the left (unless used as a short cut across the field, turning left onto a bridleway which comes out on the lane leading to How Hill). For the main walk, continue on, bearing slightly left to a junction of paths (marker post). The left-hand track offers a short cut joining up with the previous one, but the main walk continues straight on along a narrow path left at the edge of a field.

❻ Turn left onto a small lane and pass Cromes Farm. Pass two modern houses where the short cut comes in. Continue on uphill, passing Mill House with its sail-less

windmill on the left. Opposite is the How Hill Study Centre – an ornate thatched house with decorative plasterwork built in 1904 by Norwich architect Edward Boardman who lived there with his family until 1950. The gardens are only open in May during azalea time. Continue downhill to the car park of the How Hill Nature Reserve (toilets). The reserve is managed by the Broads Authority in traditional ways.

❼ Visit Toad Hole (entry free) – an enchanting marshman's cottage, built in 1728 and furnished as in Victorian times. Here you can buy tickets for visiting the nature reserve, famous for its swallow tail

The river Ant near How Hill.

butterflies and marsh harriers, or for a trip on the river. Return to the lane and follow it round, passing How Hill Farm and further on Page's Farm, to bear right at a bend where rights of way go off in either direction.

❽ At a T junction, turn left in the direction of Catfield and Potter Heigham and walk past the beautiful collection of buildings at The Laurels. For a short cut, carry on straight back into Ludham. To continue the main walk, turn right at the next crossroads to reach some houses and a garage at a crossroads with the A1062. Cross over and continue on along a lane (Lover's Lane), passing dwellings. Soon after the lane becomes a track, turn right at

a bridleway sign and make for Ludham Hall, standing starkly ahead up a broad green ride between fields. Walk ahead through the farm complex, passing the Hall to come out onto a lane.

❾ Turn left along Hall Common Road. Just past a cottage on the right is a bridleway which leads to St Benet's Abbey, just over a mile away on the river Bure. This walk continues on to a T junction.

❿ Turn left and head back in the direction of Ludham along Staithe Road, passing various interesting houses including Ludham Manor on the right.

COLTISHALL

Length: 4½ miles

Getting there: Coltishall is on the intersection of the B1150 and the B1354 midway between Norwich and North Walsham.	Parking: Free parking down Anchor Road just off the B1354 by the water meadows and river. There is alternative free parking for the Bure Valley	Walk by the old station. Map: OS Landranger 133 North East Norfolk or 134 Norwich and The Broads (GR 280197).

The lovely old buildings of Coltishall, many in red brick and thatched with Dutch gables, go back to the reign of Queen Anne or earlier, and indicate the village's importance for trade based on its situation on the upper reaches of the river Bure. The old staithe (near present-day Anchor Road) where there are several substantial houses and an old maltings would have been a scene of lively activity as wherries unloaded their cargo and took on local goods including the products of Coltishall's brewing industry. The famous wherries themselves were built in boatyards here

FOOD and DRINK

Coltishall is extremely well provided with places to eat and drink. Take your pick from: the Rising Sun on the river bank, a Chef and Brewer pub which does everything including morning coffee and tea, families welcome (telephone: 01603 737440); the 17th-century King's Head next door which does breakfast, morning coffee and food seven days a week including a Sunday roast, also bed and breakfast (telephone: 01603 737426); the ancient Red Lion in Church Street – a traditional local with excellent food and real ales including its own Couteshall Weasel (telephone: 01603 737402); the London Tavern looking down on the water meadows (telephone: 01603 737767); the Railway Tavern in Station Road which offers accommodation as well as bar meals and traditional Southwold ales, and is open all day (telephone: 01603 738316); the Norfolk Mead Hotel with secluded riverside gardens, open to non residents for morning coffee, afternoon tea, lunch and dinner (telephone: 01603 737531); Battees tearoom, open every day for morning coffee, lunches and afternoon tea.

and from here in 1912 was launched the last wherry to be built in Norfolk. Today the wherries have given way to pleasure craft. The lovely church of St John the Baptist, built mainly in the 13th century but with a 15th-century tower and porch, still retains its thatched roof. Towards the western end of the village where several roads intersect are more lovely old buildings, now housing various shops selling mainly antiques and bric-à-brac. Just further on is the old bridge where tradition has it that once a year the ghost of Sir Thomas Boleyn crosses, carrying the head of his daughter Anne, and nearby is old Horstead Mill, burned down in 1963, which marks the end of navigation on the Bure.

The river trade was ruined by the coming of the railway, and it is interesting to compare the two methods of transport. From the river and staithe, the walk climbs gently out of the village to reach the old railway line near the station. The track of the former Great Eastern Railway line has been relaid to carry narrow gauge trains between Aylsham and Wroxham with a footpath alongside which forms part of this walk. On leaving the railway line footpath, walkers pass through the delightful hamlet of St James before dropping back down to Anchor Road and Coltishall Common via lanes.

THE WALK

❶ Walk through the water meadows of Coltishall Common towards a waterside pub, keeping the river Bure on the left. The main road is on the right. Pass a boat house where all kinds of boats can be hired. The Coltishall village sign is on a grassy triangle where the road to Tunstead goes right. Cross a wooden footbridge into a large gravelled area by two pubs where there is free mooring at the staithe. Turn right through the gravelled area to Wroxham Road and turn left along it. Pass the Post Office and General Stores where there is a rights of way board. Continue on to the Dutch gabled Red Lion where the road becomes Church Street and to the church of St John the Baptist. On the

PLACES of INTEREST

Bure Valley Railway running between Aylsham and Wroxham (telephone: 01263 733858).
Wroxham Barns Craft Centre (telephone: 01603 783762).

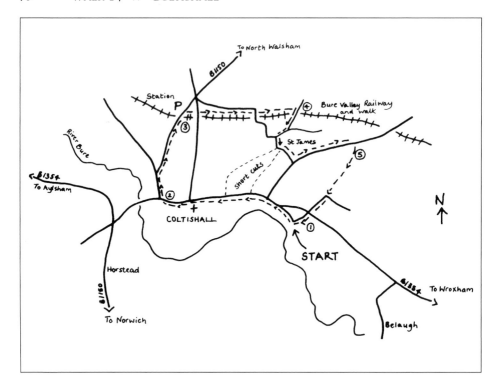

corner of Rectory Road is the Old Schoolhouse and further on is the Old School itself, built of knapped flint with an interesting roof line and old iron railings. On the left is an old maltings converted to housing. Soon, after an open green area looking down over the water meadows, you come to the centre of Coltishall where several roads meet at an island garage. High Street bears off to the left and crosses the river. A pleasant riverside walk goes off to the right from here, crossing a bridge at Little Hautbois and returning along the other side of the Bure.

❷ This walk bears right along the busy B1150 in the direction of North Walsham and Scottow, passing substantial Victorian

and Edwardian houses. Ignore the road going left to Hautbois and Skeyton and follow on up Station Road, passing the cobbled Railway Tavern.

❸ Turn left soon after the junction with Westbourne Road into the Bure Valley Walk car park by the old station, and go down steps onto the old Coltishall platform. Trains stop here on the narrow gauge Bure Valley Railway which runs from Aylsham to Wroxham, and the similarly named walk runs alongside. Turn right and walk past the station house and under a road bridge. Go under a second bridge and then a third. The track comes out of the cutting near an ivy clad railwayman's shelter.

The Bure Valley Railway line.

❹ Just before an embankment and bridge (number 1295), go down steps to the right and over a stile onto a lane bearing right into the pretty hamlet of St James. Ignore The Hill going off on the right and continue along the lane ahead, following the flint and brick wall of The Old Hall. The lane bears left where two rights of way go off (these can be used as short cuts). Continue on, following the fence of the Hall and bearing left again at a road junction to walk for some distance, passing The Hedges (B & B) on the right.

❺ Take a signposted public footpath to the right round the edge of a field. This broad grassy path swings sharply to the right to come out onto a tarmac lane. Carry on ahead, avoiding the left turn. Pass the entrance to Marlpit House as the lane meets the main road. Cross over and go down Anchor Road, bearing left to look at the interesting houses along this former staithe including converted maltings and the former pub – Anchor House – before returning to the parking area.

ELSING

Length: 2 or 3 miles

Getting there: Elsing is 2 miles south of the A1067 road halfway between Fakenham and Norwich.	Parking: Near the church and the Mermaid pub.	Map: OS Landranger 133 North East Norfolk (GR 052166).

This delightful small village near the banks of the river Wensum was once a prosperous market town. Now its few cottages and houses seem lost in tranquil, watery countryside miles from anywhere. St Mary's church, with its huge square tower, has a wealth of detail offering clues to the area's former importance. There is a most interesting brass memorial to Sir Hugh Hastings (died 1347) who built the church, together with a facsimile based on an engraving. The nave is possibly the

widest pillarless nave in England with a beautifully crafted roof of 1781. Also astonishing is the 14th-century font with a decorated canopy thought to be the oldest in the world. There are lovely black marble memorials in the chancel floor.

The walk, which is all along small lanes and is therefore suitable for pushchairs or wheelchairs, goes to 15th-century moated Elsing Hall, with foundations going back to pre-Norman times, which was built by Sir John Hast-

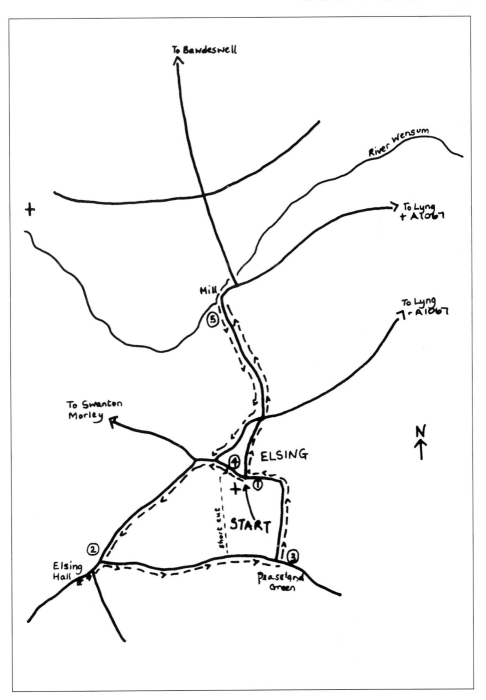

FOOD and DRINK

The Mermaid Inn with an excellent choice of real ales, a bar menu with specials and an interesting dinner menu benefits from its totally peaceful position (telephone: 01362 637640).

ings, a descendant of Sir Hugh. This romantic manor house still retains its Great Hall complete with oriel windows and has a notable garden. The route also includes the quiet lane to Elsing Mill in its charming situation on the river Wensum.

THE WALK

❶ From the church gate turn left along the lane, passing Bartles Lodge (guesthouse with day tickets for fishing) on the right. Continue on past a signposted footpath on the left where a short cut comes out. At a road junction with the colourful village sign on the right turn left and soon at another junction turn left again along Hall Road, signposted to Etling Green. From here there are broad views over tree-studded farmland. Keep on along this lane flanked with flowery banks, passing a track on the right with a view of Bylaugh church with its extraordinary tower.

❷ At a junction go straight on ahead, passing the entrance drive to Elsing Hall (gardens open on Sunday afternoons). Further on, taking the right-hand fork, there are tantalising views of this romantic building in its moated garden setting. Return up the hill, ignoring the turn to North Tuddenham on the right, then shortly turn right to Peaseland Green (Hall Farm is on the right.) Pass an almost hidden pond on the left and further on cottages on the right, one with a roadside well. At the hamlet of Peaseland Green an

Elsing's attractive village sign.

arrow marked path between two cottages on the left can be used as a short cut back to near the church.

For the main walk, continue on along the lane, passing another signposted path to the right. On the left is a good view of Elsing church over the fields. The road becomes wooded with a hidden pond on the right.

❸ Take the next turn to the left, signposted to Elsing and Lyng, along Moor Lane with more water on the left and a deep ditch on the right. Bear left at a sharp corner into Church Street, passing cottages including the Old Forge on the right and then the Mermaid pub.

PLACES of INTEREST

Norfolk Wildlife Park at Great Witchingham (telephone: 01603 872274), reached from the A1067 to the east. **Sparham Pools**, a Norfolk Wildlife Trust reserve, to the north. **North Elmham Saxon Cathedral** on the B1110 to the west.

---

❹ Turn right by the Mermaid to extend the walk by about a mile, continuing on at a crossroads and following the wiggly lane to beautiful Elsing Mill.

❺ Return back down the lane, this time turning right at the crossroads and bearing left down Back Lane to the village sign, then turning left back to the church.

HINGHAM

Length: 4 miles

Getting there: Hingham is on the B1108 between Watton and Barford and is about 5 miles west of Wymondham.

Parking: Free parking in the Market Place or on The Fairland nearby.

Map: OS Landranger 144 Thetford, Breckland and surrounding area (GR 022022).

It is quite a surprise to come across this beautiful large village of elegant houses in the middle of the south Norfolk countryside. From early times Hingham was an important place, belonging to King Athelstan, grandson of Alfred the Great. Later on in Georgian times, it became an assembly town when the surrounding country gentry built grand town houses here for use in the winter months when the roads were bad and the wind whistled round their isolated estates. The village also has connections with Abraham Lincoln. The splendid 14th-century St Andrew's church contains a bust of Lincoln, whose ancestor Samuel Lincoln

THE WALK

❶ From the 17th-century White Hart Hotel turn left and walk through the Market Place, along Norwich Road. The road curves gently to Hall Lane on the right near the Royal Oak, now a private house but still with its typical pub etched glass window. Soon after this, just before the Bay Tree pub, turn right down Stone Lane, a narrow metalled track between houses and gardens. Pass a turn to Fleeter's Hill on the right and then go through metal railings onto Bear's Lane to a junction at Mill Corner.

❷ Take the Sea Mere road, going left out of the village. Pass a few cottages and ignore the footpath signpost pointing left. Carry on to another footpath signpost on the right. Follow this path over a little bridge near a pumping station and continue on between fields. At a ditch go left, walking between the ditch on the right and a fence on the left. Continue on when the fence ends, go over a plank bridge at a knot of trees and turn right, passing between two fields with a ditch on the right. The path becomes a concrete track and meets a minor road.

For a short cut, turn right and then right again.

❸ For the main walk, turn left here and pass a track leading to Moneyhill Farm. A

FOOD and DRINK

The White Hart Hotel with accommodation, an à la carte menu and bar meals (telephone: 01953 850214); the Bay Tree with real ales and good food (telephone: 01953 850631). Lincoln's Tea and Coffee Shop, a delightful country restaurant serving everything from breakfast to cream teas, is on The Fairland.

---

was baptised here and emigrated to America in 1637 with about 200 other local people, later founding a daughter town. Other delights of the church are the 16th-century Rhineland glass and an impressive 15th-century monument (or Easter sepulchre) in red stone to Thomas Lord Morley, the local lord of the manor who fought with Henry V at the Battle of Agincourt. The Trinity chapel is also 15th century. In 1615 the rector was Robert Peck who had Puritan leanings, and joined the exodus to America. Since then the two places divided by the Atlantic have had close ties symbolised by the granite block sent from Hingham, Massachusetts in 1913 and built into a wall in the Market Place.

The peaceful lanes around the village offer lovely views over the rural landscape and the landmark tower of the church. They lead in the direction of Sea Mere, a spring fed lake, one of the sources of the river Yare, and pass the old watermill on the Deopham road. The walk ends by exploring the lanes and alleyways of the village itself to wonder at the impressive architecture, returning to the Market Place via lovely Fairland Green, for centuries the site of traditional fairs.

PLACES of INTEREST

Wymondham Abbey and heritage museum.
Wayland Wood near Watton (Norfolk Wildlife Trust).

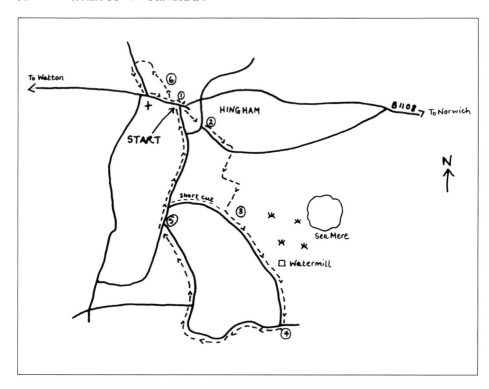

large marshy area around Sea Mere is hidden in trees on the left. The lane curves gently and offers views of the church at Deopham over the fields. Follow the lane as it bends sharply round The Watermill with views of the lovely mill pond on the left. Continue on past a pantiled cottage (Oldman's Farm) on the right, going gently uphill. The lane wiggles again and meets a junction.

❹ Turn right along an even smaller lane edged with flowery banks and mixed hedging. Follow the road to the right near the drive to Chestnut Farm and pass a junction on the left leading to Little and Great Ellingham. Continue on along Moneyhill Lane, passing Hill House on the right. Go gently downhill, enjoying the views of Hingham church.

❺ At the next T junction bear right towards Hingham. At another junction at a group of houses, ignore the right turn and continue on into Hingham along Hall Moor Road. Pass Low Road and later architectually interesting Pitt Square on the left. Ignore the right turn at Mill Corner near the former mill and continue on down Hall Lane. Pass a turning into an estate, go straight over at a little crossroads, and turn left at the main road, passing the Royal Oak again.

❻ To see some of the elegant houses of Hingham, turn right at the beginning of

The walk commences at the White Hart Hotel on the left of the picture.

Market Place, passing Beaconsfield House, Admiral's House, white painted Little London with its elegant fanlight and Quorn House in red brick. The town sign denoting the exodus to America and a pleasant wooden octagonal shelter celebrating the Queen's coronation are on the tree-edged grassy green to the left. Facing is Southernwood House with curving Dutch gables. Turn left by this, then right down a little alleyway (Talley Alley – possibly called after a candlemaker's). Bear left and then right, passing pretty cottages, into Chapel Street with the brick chapel of 1836 on the left. Turn left into Hardingham Street and then left again at the junction into Bond Street (further down this is Mansion House with beautiful two-toned brick and Dutch gables). Before this turn right into Pottle (basket) Alley which leads into The Fairland. Turn left and cross The Fairland. Cross Church Street and go along the road which passes the churchyard to look at the Manor House. Come back a little way and turn into the churchyard to visit the church, then continue on through the churchyard to exit on the other side, passing a delightful little building called The Dog (perhaps a former pub). Bear left back into the Market Place.

CASTLE ACRE

Length: 6½ miles

Getting there: Castle Acre is just off the A1065 between Fakenham and Swaffham.	**Parking:** On Stocks Green in the centre of Castle Acre.	**Map:** OS Landranger 132 North West Norfolk (GR 815151).

The pealing church bells on the day I walked were an apt reminder of the ecclesiastical importance of this ancient and attractive village, on the pilgrim route for centuries. The tree-shaded village green has the 13th-century castle gateway at one end and the church and Cluniac priory at the other with interesting shops and places of refreshment dotted between. You really

need a whole day to do justice to the extensive ruins of the castle and the priory complex and the contrasting wealth of enchanting domestic architecture.

Another contrast is in the rich wildlife areas which lie outside the village. The walk explores the wetland area of Castle Acre Common with its unique flora and fauna and crosses several fords to reach

West Acre where there are ruins of yet another priory and an interesting church. The route then passes through South Acre with a third worthwhile church before returning to Castle Acre via the banks of the river Nar, dominated by the priory ruins and the high defensive banks of the Norman castle.

THE WALK

❶ From the green walk past the church on the left. Carry on over a small road leading to South Acre, passing an ancient cottage on the left, and continue on to another junction, ignoring the left turn which leads to parking for the priory (English Heritage). Follow Priory Road as it bends to the right and then shortly go left near End House along a broad hedged track going gently downhill (Common Road).

❷ Follow the track as it bears right, then turn off it when it bears right again near a pond, and go to the left through a wooden kissing gate. Carry on along this narrow track (part of the Nar Valley Way, a 35 mile walk from King's Lynn to Gressenhall) along the edge of Castle Acre Common where the river Nar is hidden in rank growth in summer. This track (Mill Lane) carries on ahead for quite some distance

and then enters woodland belonging to the West Acre Estate through a kissing gate. After the woodland go through a metal gate into a field and continue straight across to cross a stile leading to a footbridge. Go through wooden barriers and over another footbridge. On the left is beautiful Mill House with the river Nar gushing under the mill bridge. Continue on through more wooden barriers onto a lane.

❸ Turn right here to reach a ford. Just before the ford turn left along a path ('Private Property' notice but it is a footpath) through an area of common with silver birch trees and gorse to a broad sandy track. Turn right along this to another very pretty ford. The walk can be shortened here, missing out West Acre, by turning left along the track and then shortly right into the field to follow along the hedgerow on the right (see below).

❹ To visit West Acre, cross the footbridge and continue on into West Acre village with views of West Acre priory ruins (once more important than Castle Acre) and the church on the left. At the first road junction at a grassy triangle (near the former pub), turn left to visit the pretty church with the grand priory arch next to it. Further on from the church is a large green and war memorial. At the small

The Priory.

crossroads turn right along Greenhill Lane, passing the tiny post office, and turn right at the next junction onto a more major road. Ignoring the left turn to West Acre Gardens, continue on a short way to the next crossroads and turn right again to come back to the former pub.

❺ Retrace your steps over the ford and shortly after this look out for the somewhat overgrown path to the right (see above) which goes into a field and skirts along a hedgerow on the right with the priory ruins beyond. Cross a small road (turn left for a short cut to South Acre and then Castle Acre) and continue ahead along a broad path (ignoring another path to the left through fields), going under pylon wires

ahead. Pass a barn by a wood and then, ignoring a left-hand track into a field, continue on, bearing slightly to the right up the hedgerow. At the top of a long, gentle incline the track goes right to a road.

❻ Turn left here along the edge of a field (arrow marker) and walk up the hedgerow towards Three-cocked Hat plantation. Cross over a broad track called Washpit Drove and continue on. The track wiggles a little and goes downhill gently to another cross track.

❼ Turn left along this (Petticoat Drove). The track meanders downhill past pretty Fingerhill Cottage by Fingerhill plantation. Ignore a farm track to the right

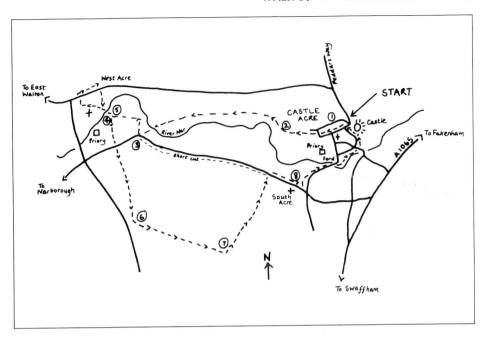

and continue on to a lane. Turn right here, passing South Acre Hall, to St George's church and the former rectory opposite.

❽ Take the next left turn, go immediately left again down a tiny lane (part of Peddars Way – an ancient 47 mile route from near Thetford to the coast at Holme), passing Church Farm and cottage, then bear right and continue on to the ford near the priory. Soon after the ford, follow the lane as it bears left, then turn immediately right into pretty water meadows over a bridge and stile. Follow the convoluted line of the river, then continue following a slightly raised causeway to reach a road near a junction. Ignore the left turn and continue up Bailey Street, passing Cuckstool Lane leading right to the castle. Bailey Street is full of attractive cottages with an old chapel to the right then the Old Red Lion (bunkhouse accommodation) with Peddars Way and Nar Valley Way maps on the wall. Go through the bailey gate and turn right to visit the castle or left back to the green.

NORTHWOLD

Length: 2 miles

Getting there: Northwold is about halfway along the A134 which runs between Thetford and the A10 south of King's Lynn.	Parking: Turn off the main road and park in the village street near the church.	Map: OS Landranger 143 Ely, Wisbech and surrounding area (GR 755970).

Northwold stands on an outcrop of chalk and the architecture of the village reflects this. There are some large 17th and 18th-century houses built in a variety of materials including chalk blocks, and delightful knapped flint and chalk built cottages, occasionally colour washed and some with cinder galletting (small lumps of cinder incorporated into the structure). Flint towered St Andrew's church was associated with Hugh of Northwold (Bishop of Ely from 1229 to 1254) and is exceptionally fine. The 13th-century arcades, some with carved capitals, lead up to the painted angels and flowers of the roof. The beautiful Easter sepulchre of

1480, which escaped destruction during the Reformation, is reputedly the largest in the country. The remains of an old market cross stand on a bend in the main street. A curious hamlet called Little London, ½ mile east of the village, has some very old and interesting buildings.

This short walk concentrates on the architecture in the two parallel main streets of the village. Hall Lane, joining these two streets, has a school, almshouses and a village hall of around 1874, all given by Caroline Amelia Norman, wife of the rector of the day. She was the daughter of John Julius Augerstein, a rich Russian Jew who lived at nearby Weeting Hall and whose collection of pictures went to found the National Gallery. The walk finishes with a pleasant tramp along old drove lanes through the fields where tracks lead north to the river Wissey.

THE WALK
❶ Face the large derelict building opposite the church and walk to the left along the High Street, ignoring Church Lane which goes to the right. Pass some very pretty chalk and flint houses. At the end of the village a wide track (Riverside becoming Highmoor Drove) goes to the left over a ford to a bridge crossing the river Wissey and on to the village of Foulden for a pleasant rural detour. About ½ mile further on along the main road are the attractive old houses and cottages of Little London,

again a detour from the main walk.

❷ For the main walk, just before Riverside take a turn to the right down Hovell's Lane (note the lovely old barn walls on the right), called after an old moated mansion visible in aerial photographs in what is now the sports field. Soon, turn right down Cross Lane, passing cottages of mixed ages with open fields on the left. At the next crossroads go straight over and carry on along School Lane. Pass Victorian (1874) almshouses on the right and then the village hall of the same period. Ignore the lane which goes right and continue straight on with the bell-towered Victorian school (much increased) on the left, named after its benefactor, Mrs Norman. At the next crossroads continue on again along Pinfold Lane, passing chalk buildings and some flint cottages on the left. The lane passes through more open country then bends to the right. Follow it down to meet the main village street with some lovely chalk cottages on the left. To the left is West End with yet more interesting old houses.

❸ However, this walk goes to the right towards the old market cross situated where the road widens on a bend. Follow the bend of the road and very shortly turn off left down a green lane (public footpath signpost) and walk out through fields

St Andrew's church.

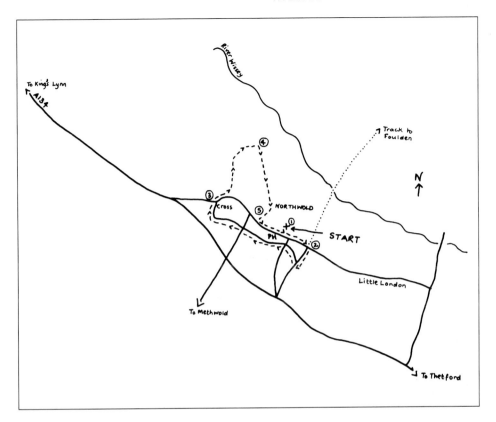

dotted with trees. As the lane bends left, go to the right and cross a footbridge, then bear immediately left along the stream for a short distance. The broad grassy track then bears to the right away from the stream with a fence on the right and views over to the church tower.

❹ At a T junction of tracks turn right and follow Common Drove, a very broad track, back in the direction of the village with fine views of the church again. The track bears to the right to cross a bridge by a ford, passing an interesting chalk block and brick mill building on the left.

❺ Come out onto the main street again and turn left, passing the post office and village shop, and then the Crown Inn, to reach the church.

SAXLINGHAM NETHERGATE
Length: 5¼ miles

Getting there: Saxlingham Nethergate is about 7 miles south of Norwich, a mile from the A140 road between Norwich and Ipswich.	Parking: To one side of the main street towards the war memorial.	Map: OS Landranger 134 Norwich and The Broads (GR 229973).

Although not far from Norwich, Saxlingham Nethergate seems lost in a remote and timeless world. One of the first areas in Norfolk to be designated a Conservation Area, streets of attractive cottages and reed thatched houses meet at the award winning war memorial. At the heart of the village the lovely church, St Mary's, sits on the edge of a green between two fine houses – 17th-century timbered Old Hall and the Old Rectory (18th century) designed by Sir John Soane.

The surrounding countryside, set in the valley of the river Tas, offers views over a web of fields and woods laced with hedged lanes, leading to small hamlets and

FOOD and DRINK

The West End pub at Saxlingham Thorpe (on the main A140 by the Foxhole turn) is open all day every day from 12 noon and serves a selection of food including Yorkshire puddings with six different fillings (telephone: 01508 470005).

ancient farms. The area has revealed many archaeological finds, from the Neolithic period through the Iron Age to Romano-British remains. The landscape is studded with churches, some vibrant with life and interest, some gaunt and derelict, and some marked only by a grass covered mound of stones. The walk passes the ruins of ancient St Mary Magdalene church to reach the old houses strung out along the edges of wide, tree-hung Saxlingham Green before returning to Saxlingham Nethergate via field paths and more small lanes.

THE WALK

❶ Leaving the post office and shop near the war memorial on the left, walk up the main street along the pavement, passing pretty houses and cottages. Over the road are white railings bordering the stream running alongside the Old Rectory grounds, and further on the small metal bridge over which the walk returns. Turn left off the main street along a small lane by farm barns. Pass a few houses and then the undenominational chapel and go out into the countryside. At a road junction turn right, and then almost immediately right again along leafy Long Lane. A break in the hedgerow offers views over the village of Newton Flotman flanked by its church

over the valley on the right.

❷ At a sharp bend to the right, turn left off the metalled road, ignore the wide track going ahead and take the narrow tree-hung sunken track to the left which eventually comes out by a cottage garden onto another small lane in the hamlet of Foxhole. Turn left (Windy Lane). Ignore the drive to Woodhouse Farm on the right and just further on, where the lane bends to the left, bear right along a fairly wide track, signposted with a Boudicca's Way marker (a 38 mile walk from Norwich to Diss). Ignore a signposted footpath to the right. Further on an unsigned but obvious path goes to the left back to Saxlingham Nethergate (a short cut to Pitt's Hill where a right turn leads back to the war memorial). The main walk continues on here, downhill to reach a broad signposted cross track (another short cut to the left). Cross this and continue on ahead along a sunken narrow track which bears right near trees and continues ahead along a field baulk towards a wood which masks the remains of old St Mary Magdalene church where many path converge.

❸ Bear left and continue to follow the edge of the wood (and remains of the old church wall) round to the right to join a wide track. Ignore paths to right and left

PLACES of INTEREST

All the attractions of nearby **Norwich** (Tourist Office telephone: 01603 666071). **Caistor St Edmund Roman town**, just south of Norwich, off the A140.

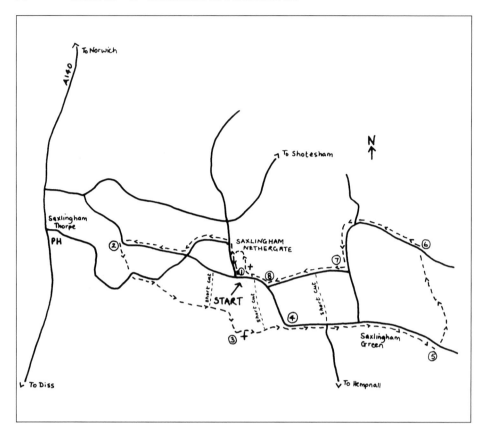

(short cut), and turn left along another track leading towards a thatched house on the road.

❹ Turn right along the road and follow it as it bears left. Ignore the path which goes to the right. Pass a red brick house on the bend. Where the larger road bears to the right to Hempnall at a cluster of pretty cottages on a green, continue on ahead along a minor road (a short cut path to the left leads to Hall Lane which then goes left back to the village). The main walk follows the minor road through Saxlingham Green edged with lovely timber-framed former farmhouses. Chequers Lane to the left provides another short cut meeting Hall Lane. Continue on the main walk, passing 17th-century Queen Anne Saxlingham Hall on the left. Further on, almost opposite a footpath signpost to the right, look for a similar one on the left a little way over the green.

❺ Walk straight across a field towards a hedgerow, turning left along this to a signpost by a ditch. Continue on along the edge of the field, keeping the ditch to the right, in the direction of a pantiled barn. Continue on past the barn along the edge

The 17th-century timbered Old Hall.

of the field to reach a road through a signposted gap in the hedge.

❻ Turn left along Wash Lane. After some distance the road comes to a junction. Turn left along Wood Lane (ford when wet). Follow the road round to the right and left. A signposted footpath ahead eventually leads back to the path behind the church which the main walk joins later. For this walk, however, continue along Chequers Lane to the left.

❼ Near a splendid avenue of trees which curves off in the direction of Saxlingham Hall, turn right along tiny Hall Lane. Continue past footpaths signposted to the left and right to come out on the main road through the village.

❽ Turn right, passing the school, to reach Church Green and the carved village sign. Go through a kissing gate into the churchyard. The church is mainly 14th century with lovely medieval stained glass, some of which came from ruined St Mary Magdalene. The tower has a splendid clock face and sun dial and there are some fine carved gravestones. Continue on through the churchyard and go through a wooden kissing gate, along a path next to a field. At a cross track turn left, passing a stile where the path next from the Chequers Lane corner comes in, and carry on to cross a small metal bridge onto the road. Turn left back to the parking place.

KENNINGHALL

Length: 2½ miles

Getting there: Kenninghall is on the B1113 about 3 miles north of South Lopham which is on the A1066 road between Thetford and Diss.	Parking: In the Market Place.	Map: OS Landranger 144 Thetford, Breckland and surrounding area (GR 037861).

Present-day Kenninghall with its few streets of picturesque houses and cottages, leading on to the sleepy Market Place, gives little indication of its great importance in times gone by. There have been archaeological finds in the area dating back to the Stone and Bronze Ages, as well as an Anglo-Saxon burial ground and a Romano-British urn burial. A banked earthwork at Candles Yard is said to be a dwelling place of Queen Boudicca of the Iceni, who died in AD 62 and is reputedly buried at nearby Quidenham. In the early 16th century, the Duke of Norfolk

FOOD and DRINK

The Red Lion opposite the church dates back to 1722 and offers a good selection of real ales and some interesting food (closed on Monday and Tuesday lunchtimes, telephone: 01953 887849). The White Horse in Market Place is open every day and has a good range of beers and a limited but adequate menu which is changed every week (telephone: 01953 887379). The post office at Quidenham, 1 mile north of Kenninghall, serves coffee, light lunches and cream teas by a wood burning stove or on a pleasant terrace at the rear (telephone: 01953 887200).

the left is the Particular Pottery housed in an attractive flint chapel of 1807 belonging to the Particular Baptists and standing in its original graveyard – one of three chapels in the village. Further along the raised causeway is pargeted Church Farmhouse and then St Mary's church itself with the Red Lion pub opposite. The fine tower was built in the 15th century with a later parapet, and the entrance porch has a lovely Norman doorway carved with animals including a riderless white horse believed to be Saxon.

built a splendid palace at Kenninghall, one wing of which still exists as a farmhouse to the east of the village.

This short walk explores the fascinating and varied architecture of the village itself before venturing out into the surrounding countryside with views over pastoral scenery. The walk can be extended by going north along a country lane which leads to the hamlet of Quidenham with its church with an unusual round tower and spire, and a Carmelite monastery in Quidenham Park.

THE WALK

Streets radiate out from the central Market Place which has the 16th-century White Horse pub on the north side near a newsagents and grocery store. Over the square is the post office housed in an old building with crow-stepped gables, and a garage.

❶ From the Market Place walk along West Church Street, ignoring the first little turn to the left. The cottages on the right have gardens going down to the beck which runs under the Market Place. Up the bank to

❷ Just after the church, turn left along a broad track leading past Old Mill House on the right. Follow the track right at Mill House and then where the broad track bears left at a footpath marker post continue ahead along a narrow path between two fields. This comes out onto a broad grassy track passing intensive feeding units. The track turns right here and meets a farm road. Bear right at this, going sharp right and then left to meet a more main road by a farmhouse.

❸ Turn right along the road, passing some scattered cottages and then a tiny derelict chapel on the left. More pretty houses and

PLACES of INTEREST

The Particular Pottery in Kenninghall, a working pottery and gallery (telephone: 01953 888476). Banham Zoo (telephone: 01953 887771), reached along the B1113 to the north. Banham Cider in the Appleyard opposite the zoo (telephone: 01953 888593). Bressingham Steam Museum and Gardens (telephone: 01379 688133), off the A1066 east of South Lopham.

Quidenham church.

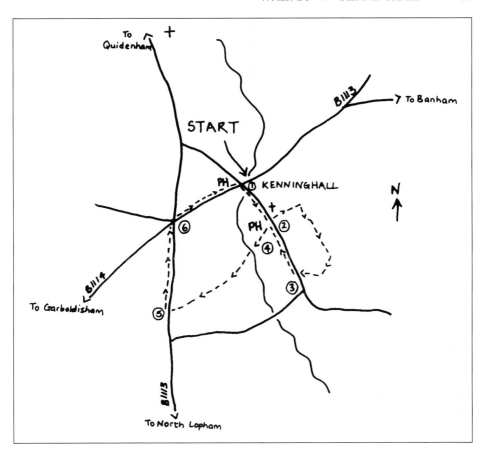

cottages line West Church Street as it leads back to the centre of the village.

❹ Just before the Red Lion pub, turn left along an alley which then turns into a sunken grassy lane leading downhill between banks (a ford when wet). At a crossroads of tracks, go straight ahead along a narrow path with a field on the right and a hedge running most of the length on the left. This path broadens out and passes more intensive feeding units to meet the B1113 road.

❺ Turn right along this, passing a colour washed cottage on the brow of the hill. Ignore the signposted footpath opposite this and continue on along the road, passing an electricity sub-station and then the playing field. Just past the red brick school with its horse weathervane you come to a junction of five roads with the Kenninghall village sign standing on the green opposite.

❻ Turn right along the main road, crossing over the lane leading to the school and the Memorial Hall. Pass an egg packing station to the right and continue on back to the Market Place.